JB JOSSEY-BASS™
A Wiley Brand

92 Strategies for Marketing Planned Gifts

Scott C. Stevenson, Editor

WILEY

978-1-118-69045-1   ISBN

978-1-118-70384-7   ISBN (online)

92 Strategies
For Marketing Planned Gifts

Published by

Stevenson, Inc.

P.O. Box 4528 • Sioux City, Iowa • 51104
Phone 712.239.3010 • Fax 712.239.2166
www.stevensoninc.com

92 Strategies for Marketing Planned Gifts

Table of Contents

Table of Contents

92 Strategies for Marketing Planned Gifts

1. Five Tips for Making Planned Giving Work for You

Officials at Lawrence University (Appleton, WI) have spent the last two years revamping planned giving efforts. Through that process, Associate Vice President of Major and Planned Giving Barbara Stack says she has one rule of thumb when it comes to creating and improving planned giving programs: "Keep it simple. Ninety percent of planned gifts are made through bequests, so focus energy on promoting them."

In promoting bequests, Stack says, keep this top-of-mind: "The most compelling messages for bequest promotion . . . focus on legacy, dreams and ensuring that the donor's values live on through the organizations they care about."

Stack identifies five specific guidelines that Lawrence University officials are using to make their planned giving programs stronger:

1. **Talk to younger donors about retirement assets.** Stack says this allows them to consider your organization earlier in life, which means they are less likely to need convincing later.
2. **Remember that getting started in planned giving doesn't need to be expensive.** "There is so much information, good material, solid advice and quality vendors in our line of work," she says. "Don't get caught up in the fancy tools unless you have trusted advisors who will work with you to do it right (e.g., CGAs, trusts, real estate, etc.)."
3. **Put your donors and your mission front and center.** "This is the best and most effective way to raise funds generally, but especially with planned gifts," says Stack. "Allow your best marketing partners — those who have already 'done it' — to feel great about their decision by allowing them to share their philanthropic journey. Allow the beneficiaries of your mission to express their own thanks to help illustrate what gifts accomplish."
4. **Have a quality web presence** and piggyback your planned giving message with other logical communications from your organization.
5. **Measure your planned giving efforts by tracking meaningful contacts and visits with prospects and donors.** Provide stellar follow-up and stewardship, and ensure you have the knowledge and resources to respond to inquiries.

"Most importantly, do not lose sight of why you are doing what you are doing," says Stack. "Planned gifts are not great because of tax advantages or glossy brochures or newsletters. They are another means to an end of fulfilling a donor's wishes to help your organization, because it matters to them. If you always focus on the mission and helping donors find ways to support that mission . . . you will be doing your best work for your cause and your donors."

Source: Barbara J. Stack, Associate Vice President of Major and Planned Giving, Lawrence University, Appleton, WI. E-mail: barbara.j.stack@lawrence.edu

Focus on Professional Advisors Helpful, Too

The recent planned giving program revamp at Lawrence University (Appleton, WI) calls for engaging and educating local professional advisors such as wealth and trust managers, estate planning attorneys, tax and insurance professionals who can positively influence and assist their clients with charitable-giving decisions. Barbara Stack, associate vice president of major and planned giving, shares a specific example of how this effort is already making an impact:

"A local attorney who knew that his client had made a provision in his will for Lawrence had become more educated and interested in Lawrence's programs because of our professional advisor outreach. The attorney shared information about the amount required to endow a scholarship, which was a little more than what the client had already planned in his estate, but which is something the client was very excited about doing when it was explained to him.

"The client updated his will, ensuring the estate provision would meet the endowed scholarship. He also shared that news with Lawrence, allowing us to thank him and discuss priorities for his scholarship gift, which were documented for the future. We expect this type of scenario to be the end result of the efforts we are making to form meaningful relationships with these professionals."

Planned Giving Requires Donor-centric Focus

Barbara Stack, associate vice president of major and planned giving at Lawrence University (Appleton, WI), discusses some of the challenges university officials have encountered and changes they have made through a recent two-year renovation of the university's planned giving efforts:

What sort of unique things are you working on in the area of planned giving?

"We developed a unique peer-outreach approach to our program, giving it a distinct Lawrence 'face.' We have about 35 volunteers who are members of our legacy recognition society who assist us in promoting planned giving to their fellow alumni and constituents who live in their regions across the country. The members help us raise visibility and recruit new members by hosting small parties with prospects, writing notes thanking new members, providing testimonials at events and in printed and electronic materials, serving in leadership roles for planned gift promotion as they approach milestone reunions and advising us on our website and printed marketing materials."

What have been your biggest challenges in terms of planned giving and how have you worked to overcome them?

"Our challenges stem from those things we cannot control, like fiscal caution resulting from the recent economic climate. This has provided us with both challenge and opportunity. Over the past couple of years, our donors and prospects have generally been skittish about making any changes to their financial or long-term plans, because they are uncertain about the future. We've addressed those concerns by being patient, continuing to focus on our mission and assuring donors that we work on their timeline and will be here when they're ready. At the same time, our donors have been more receptive to discussing how they might accomplish their philanthropic vision and dreams without jeopardizing their current situation. Due to these conversations, we were able to help our planned-gift donors and prospects feel satisfaction by participating in our capital campaign through joining our legacy society and estimating future gifts that could be counted in our campaign."

2. Build Solid Relationships With Insurance Agents

Whenever your organization is named both owner and beneficiary of a paid-up life insurance policy — or the donor willingly makes annual gifts equal to insurance premiums until the policy is paid up — that's a welcomed major gift. And that's why you should work to build mutually beneficial relationships with insurance agents who sell life insurance. Once they understand the win-win rationale behind a charitable life insurance gift, they will act more assertively on your behalf.

To focus on relationship building with this agents-of-wealth profession, map out an ongoing plan that may include any of the following strategies:

1. Host a quarterly breakfast for area insurance agents with a portion of the program dedicated to some topic they will find to be of value (e.g., trends impacting the insurance profession, effective sales techniques) and the remaining part of the program directed to educating attendees on your organization and its planned giving program.

2. Whenever a donor gives an insurance policy and grants permission to publicize the gift, don't forget to make mention of the insurance agent and company who helped make the gift possible. A little public recognition will go a long way in keeping that agent/company working on your behalf.

3. Don't be hesitant about including names of insurance agents (and other agents of wealth who have assisted your cause — trust departments, attorneys, CPAs) among your list of volunteers in your annual report and other publications. Do seek permission first, however, since some professionals prefer to help in more anonymous ways.

3. Three Things to Do on Your Way to $35 Million

Director of Planned Gifts Steven Rosenblum, Saint Louis Zoo (Saint Louis, MO) can tout some great stats when it comes to planned giving. Zoo development staff, including Rosenblum, have raised $28 million towards a $35 million goal since announcing their Living Promise Campaign in June 2008. They created 3 endowed positions (ranging in scope from $1.5 M to $3M) and 23 endowed funds ($50,000 minimum, ranging up to $1.3M), and helped the Saint Louis Zoo Endowment Trust grow from zero to $38 million.

They have also increased the number of Heritage Society members — donors who have included the zoo in their estate plans — from 140 to nearly 300.

Rosenblum is charged with helping to set internal goals, along with one other director and the vice president for external affairs. Each development officer is charged with a certain number of visit and tour goals, as well as an achievable fundraising goal. These goals include stewardship of a prospect pool ranging from 150 to 300 donors who are annual, major gift and planned giving prospects. Staff members use quarterly reports to remain up-to-date on meetings, tours and dollars raised to date.

As a result, Rosenblum knows quite a bit about what does and doesn't work. Here, he shares advice on some of the things he has learned in the process of posting impressive numbers:

- Work on increasing your bequest society. Find the low-hanging fruit and get them to join. Revisit your committed donors to find out more about them and their wishes.

- Be sure to continually market your program by piggybacking on current materials and mailings.

- If you have a good base, consider a gift annuity program and other more sophisticated gifts like remainder and lead trusts.

Rosenblum says relying on a technical explanation of gifts is a definite no-no. "It often overwhelms donors. I have found that a more generic message, highlighting the benefits of giving and the direct link to our mission work best. We can follow up with a more technical discussion in person afterward."

Source: Steven Rosenblum, Director of Planned Gifts, Saint Louis Zoo, St. Louis, MO. E-mail: Rosenblum@stlzoo.org

4. Facilitate Planned Gifts With Online Gift Calculator

Some donors like hammering out the details of a gift with development officers. Others prefer to plan a gift as thoroughly as possible in private before sharing their intentions. Online gift calculators are one way to accommodate this preplanning kind of donor.

Gift calculators allow donors to figure and refigure gift outcomes like tax deductibility and income generated by revenue-producing tools like charitable gift annuities.

If you think an online gift calculator might enhance your planned giving website, take a look at the examples below.

- **Harvard University** uses a calculator (http://alumni. harvard.edu/give/planned-giving/resources-events/ calculator) that allows a user to choose any of a dozen types of gifts (pooled income, gift annuity, etc.), and it automatically adjusts the information fields required for each.

- **Case Western Reserve University** maintains its own in-house Planned Giving Calculation Center (http://www. case.edu/giving/planned/tools/giftcalculator.html), which

is structured around two sets of services — a simple interface designed to provide prospective donors with approximate deduction amounts, and a more advanced one designed to help planned giving advisors calculate more precise figures. The latter generates detailed reports that can be used to support IRS filings. Both offer clickable dialog boxes that thoroughly explain the information needed in each input field.

- **The Houston Grand Opera** expands on the idea of planned gift calculators by offering a range of personal finance calculators (http://www.legacy.vg/ houstongrandopera/articles/40.html) for areas like cash flow, taxation, insurance and retirement. Included under these categories are some twenty planning questions like, "What is my current net worth?", "How much retirement income can my IRA provide?" and "How much life insurance do I need?" Each question is linked to its own calculator, with the number of required information fields ranging from two to several dozen.

5. Techniques to Strengthen Emotional Ties With Donors

One of the key generators of fundraising is emotion, says Marshall Howard, founder of Marshall Howard and Associates (Canoga Park, CA), a consulting firm that emphasizes strategic communications as a way to increase organizational fundraising capacity.

"People give to people; people don't give to causes," Howard explains. "If you can't connect with that donor, it doesn't matter how important your organization's mission is."

So how do you steer your communications with major donors away from the transactional and towards the emotional? Here, Howard offers three successful methods.

✓ The first fundamental of creating emotion is to be curious about other people. "For me to communicate with you, I need to know who you are as a person first," says Howard. "When you ask questions and you're curious about who that person is, I call it a compassionate conversation." Ask the donor how he got started in his particular industry, how long she's lived in town (particularly when making an in-home visit), etc.

✓ When speaking with the donor by phone, don't just talk business. "You can build rapport on the phone just as you can in person," says Howard. "You just can't do it on the business level, because then you only know me in a role and I only know you in a role, and we become very guarded." You may feel compelled to keep a phone call short so as not to make the donor feel like you're wasting his or her time, but if you lead the discussion around to a favorite topic, the donor won't feel that way.

✓ When turned down for a major gift, call and ask why. "Grantmakers tell me, 'You know, I really appreciate when people call me and ask me why they didn't get the grant.' That's part of the growth process in a relationship." A good way to phrase it: "I'm curious, why were we denied the gift? I'd love to come over and talk to you for a few minutes."

Source: Marshall Howard, Founder, Marshall Howard and Associates, Canoga Park, CA.
E-mail: mhoward@marshallhoward.com

6. Learn How Storytelling Can Close More Gifts

How often do you use personal anecdotes to make a point during the solicitation process?

Storytelling can be a powerful tool in motivating others to give. Besides making the person with whom you're speaking more comfortable, personal stories make an impression. They make the experience more memorable.

Incorporate personal stories into your meetings with prospects by following these steps:

1. **Know what you want the story to accomplish.** Is the story meant to inspire? Is it intended to prove a point? Describing a personal anecdote with an unrelated conclusion only serves to confuse or annoy someone.
2. **Rely on your real-life experiences as you develop a menu of stories from which to draw.** Your stories will convey a greater sense of passion, if they come from past experiences that had an impression on you.
3. **Practice by telling the story to colleagues and friends.** Hearing yourself share it with others will help you to convey the message with ease and allow you to embellish or emphasize key points. Your style should be relaxed and conversational.
4. **Conclude your story with a sentence that ties it back to the here and now.** If, for instance, you have just shared a story about a woman who derived great joy by establishing an endowed scholarship, make that story relevant to the individual by saying something like, "Knowing you as I do, I can only imagine how excited and fulfilled you would be by establishing your own scholarship fund."

Draw From Past Experiences

Develop a menu of personal anecdotes from which to choose, depending on the situation and what you intend to accomplish during the meeting. Draw from any of these or other past experiences:

- ❑ Something you experienced involving a person you greatly respect.
- ❑ A simple statement or act from a child who made a big impression on you.
- ❑ A difficult and trying experience which, after time, had positive consequences.
- ❑ An act of monumental proportions that had long-lasting positive effects.
- ❑ A quiet, unassuming experience that may have gone unnoticed by most, but left a lasting impression on you.
- ❑ The evolution of another donor's major gift and the resulting benefits to both the donor and your charity.

7. Take Life Income Gifts on a Case-by-case Basis

"The most important tools for building a sustainable life income gift program are ample time and strategic relationship building," says Director of Capital Gifts and Planned Giving Michelle Staes, Agnes Scott College (Decatur, GA). "My experience has shown stewardship and cultivation of life income donors are most effective on a case-by-case basis."

Staes has found that for life income donors who wish to remain private about their giving, stewardship may include a handwritten note highlighting how the gift will assist the mission of the college and/or inviting the donor to an on-campus event, while honoring the donor's wish not to be publicly acknowledged.

For donors who are comfortable with public acknowledgment, Staes says featuring them in marketing materials about life income gifts is very effective. "Such stewardship encourages others to give in a similar manner and actually puts the donor back into the pipeline for another planned gift. The marketing piece provides the opportunity for the donor to share what the college means to her in print with a large audience of friends, family, students, faculty and board members."

Having alumnae identify other alumnae as planned giving prospects can also be very effective, says Staes. "Alumnae tend to know each other best, and are thus, wonderful sources of information with the ability to make connections for development officers."

Perhaps the best advice Staes can offer about life income gifts is this: "It is important to build the relationship with a prospect, not expecting an immediate positive response to the idea of a planned gift. A prospect needs to hear the information often, from various sources."

Source: Michelle S. Staes, JD, Director of Capital Gifts and Planned Giving, Office of Development, Agnes Scott College, Decatur, GA. E-mail: mstaes@agnesscott.edu

8. Provide Preemptive Stewardship to Suspected Donors

Studies indicate that for every supporter who shares his or her bequest intentions, two or more choose not to do so. These silent donors are an important reservoir of support, and finding ways to steward them will pay great dividends. Not only does the average planned gift range from $35,000 to $70,000 in the United States, gifts from donors who share their intentions tend to be about twice as large as those from donors who do not.

How do fundraisers go about unlocking this hidden support? The key is reaching out to people who you suspect have included your organization in their estate plans, just like you would to known major donors, says Katherine Swank, senior consultant at Target Analytics, a Blackbaud company (Charleston, SC).

"Major donors and planned gift donors are surprisingly similar. Both are affluent. They just differ in how they feel about their wealth," she says. "Major donors feel like they can give it away and typically expect recognition in return. Planned gift donors are more financially and informationally conservative."

The first step in adding a stewardship element to your planned gifts program, Swank says, is building a suspect pool based on profiling, modeling and analytics. More sophisticated organizations will often choose a sophisticated analysis of their donor base.

Once identified, these suspects need to be treated like known major donors. "Basically you act as if things are the way you want them to be," says Swank. "Instead of waiting for people to come forward, you treat them as if they have already informed you, which creates space for the relationship to grow and deepen."

This involves giving planned gift suspects the kinds of perks major donors receive, things like inviting them to tours and luncheons, giving them access to leadership, including them in special mailings and adding handwritten notes on reports and communications.

Swank says it also involves providing recognition in a way that will be comfortable to silent donors. "Profiling the impact of anonymous gifts will let silent donors know that others are stepping forward to make quiet gifts; send the message that you will not publicize their name unless they want you to."

Source: Katherine Swank, Senior Consultant, Target Analytics, Charleston, SC. E-mail: Katherine.swank@blackbaud.com

9. Seek Donor Testimonials

Give major donors a voice to recognize them and encourage others to give as well.

When a donor documents a planned gift to the Roland Park Country School (RPCS), Baltimore, MD, school officials ask for a brief testimonial, says Ginny Wood Delauney, assistant director of development and director of gift planning.

"We like to hear the donors' own voices, so we try not to alter what they write," Delauney says. "I usually send them a couple of examples, so that they have an idea of what I would like from them.

"It is nice to show a variety of donors as well as an array of deferred gift types," she adds. "Most donors seem pleased to be asked to write something and hope that their testimonial will encourage others to make a planned gift to the school."

In addition to posting the testimonials on the school's planned giving Web page, school officials spotlight donors in magazines and planned giving materials. "We write more in-depth profiles on donors . . . for a number of reasons," says Delauney. "It could be because someone has recently passed away, their gift has been realized, and we want to acknowledge and honor them. It might also be because we want to highlight the particular planned gift vehicle that the donor chooses, such as a charitable remainder trust or an irrevocable bequest."

Source: Ginny Wood Delauney, Assistant Director of Development, Director of Gift Planning, Roland Park Country School, Baltimore, MD. E-mail: delauneyg@rpcs.org

Roland Park Country School (Baltimore, MD) features major donor testimonials on its website, including this from a 1998 alum:

"It was because of my experiences and education at RPCS that I became the person I am today.

"It is for this reason that I wanted to give the School as much as I could afford, so I made a deferred gift in the form of a life insurance policy.

"Charitable life insurance policies provide a tax deduction to the donor while supporting RPCS in a most affordable way.

"It makes me proud that I have taken the initiative to help guarantee greater opportunities for future students."

10. Maximize Time Spent Nurturing Planned Gifts

What can planned gifts officers do to make the most of their time? Here's how several planned gift veterans responded:

1. Get to know agents of wealth: attorneys, trust officers, accountants and insurance agents who can help to broaden your efforts.

2. Keep building and fine-tuning your mailing list of prospect names who receive regular information on planned gift issues from your cause.

3. Properly steward existing planned gift donors.

4. Offer various types of estate planning seminars that will put you in touch with likely prospects and enhance your planned gift credentials.

5. Set challenging but realistic planned gift goals for yourself (e.g., number of calls per week, number of new planned gift expectancies per year, number of estate planning seminars).

6. Initiate or expand on your planned gifts club or society that recognizes those who have made planned gift provisions.

7. Faithfully publicize bequests and other forms of planned gifts as a way to recognize donors and promote similar gifts.

8. Stay abreast of laws, tax implications and other issues that impact planned gifts and nonprofits.

11. Seek Out Ambassadors in Wealthy Neighborhoods

If your community has residential areas that represent greater wealth, work to identify existing donors from those sections to serve as centers of influence in an ongoing capacity. Whether they become part of a major gifts committee, or you choose to work with each on an individual basis, these ambassadors — who already have a history of giving to your organization and believe in your mission — can help to:

1. Identify potential donors from their assigned territories.

2. Initiate research efforts, providing useful information on neighborhood prospects.

3. Make introductions and cultivate new friendships with these residents.

4. Accompany staff on solicitation calls.

5. Steward residents from their assigned areas who have made gifts to your organization.

12. Convince Centers of Influence To Promote Your Cause

Is one of your objectives to promote planned gifts? Then it's in your best interest to convince centers of influence to promote your charity, within ethical limits, to those who use their services.

Before these centers of influence can be convinced to promote your cause, they must first believe in your mission and goals themselves. So how do you compete for their loyalty among a sea of other worthy causes also vying for their attention?

First, you enlist and regularly involve centers of influence in your planned gifts program and help them to visualize what the realization of planned gifts will do to change your organization and benefit those you serve. As they buy into your dreams, they will want to help turn those dreams into reality.

Second, through your planned gifts committee or another planned gifts advisory group, ask them to help identify planned gift prospects. Meet regularly, both individually and one-on-one, to:

• Identify planned gift prospects.
• Rate and screen planned gift prospects.
• Determine appropriate ways to approach the prospects.
• Discuss ways in which individual planned gifts might be funded.
• Review funding opportunities that may be of interest to prospects.

Involving centers of influence in these ways will bring your nonprofit to the forefront and multiply your efforts toward generating planned gifts.

13. Don't Overlook the Profitable Possibilities of Retained Life Estate Gifts

Assess Property Details Before Accepting Retained Life Estate Gifts

How does a nonprofit organization go about accepting real estate as a gift?

"The first step is ascertaining the basic details of the property, primarily its value, location, zoning and marketability," says Phillip Purcell, vice president for planned giving and endowment stewardship, Ball State University Foundation (Muncie, IN). "If the charity finds interest, it would then need to undertake environmental audits, property inspections and title review."

The nonprofit should pay for elements that protect the nonprofit, and the donor should pay for elements that protect the donor, Purcell says. The donor, for example, should cover the appraisal, because it is the basis for the donor's claim of a charitable deduction. The charity should usually pay for environmental review, property inspections, deed preparation and title review, because it needs to know those tasks have been completed professionally and accurately.

Agreements on who pays property taxes, insurance and maintenance costs should be formalized, he says. Because a property could be liquidated or at risk if taxes or insurance are neglected, the charity should try to include in the agreement an annual verification of the donor's ability to pay these ongoing costs.

"Contingencies should also be spelled out," Purcell says. "What if the donor wants to sell the property? What if the donor moves out and wants to rent the property? What if the donor decides to give up the remaining life estate? The charity has a stake in these transactions and should make sure its rights and prerogatives are clearly defined."

Throughout the process, know that there are circumstances in which a nonprofit should turn down the offer of real estate, Purcell says.

"People often have overly optimistic opinions of the value of their home. Some also offer property they can't sell themselves, figuring they will at least get a deduction for it," he says. "The bottom line is that a property should not be accepted if it cannot be sold at a profit within a reasonable amount of time. Real estate with environmental issues like major asbestos or contamination trouble should also be refused."

Nonprofit professionals who wish to pursue gifts of real estate should first educate themselves by consulting legal counsel and real estate professionals, Purcell says. They should then establish policies and procedures on how real estate gifts will be handled, and have their board of directors review and approve the policies. Most charities reserve the final decision on real estate gifts for the board so board members can ensure due diligence has occurred.

Every real estate gift is uniquely challenging, says Phillip Purcell, vice president for planned giving and endowment stewardship, Ball State University Foundation (Muncie, IN).

Purcell answers questions and shares insights on a class of donations known as retained life estate (RLE) gifts, which the planned giving expert says is a gift option nonprofit organizations often overlook:

What is a retained life estate gift?

"It's an irrevocable gift of the remainder interest in a donor's personal residence or farm. The donor keeps a life estate, retains the right to live on and use it during his or her lifetime, and on death it passes to the charitable institution (see illustration)."

Content not available in this edition

How does that differ from bequeathing a home in a will?

"Revocability is one of the big differences. Bequests are revocable, and some people like the flexibility this offers. They like having more control over the home or farm, and being able to sell it should they need the cash. RLE gifts are irrevocable and less flexible in some ways, but offer many advantages as well."

What are some of these advantages?

"Primarily tax benefits. Because the gift is irrevocable, the donor can take an income tax charitable deduction (based on their age and the value of the property) in the year the gift is made, rather than waiting until the end of life. The transfer is not subject to capital gains tax, and the property passes free of federal estate tax as long as the life estate is left to a charitable institution.

"From the charity's perspective, a major benefit is the absence of probate. Because RLE is irrevocable, it is not subject to probate and therefore escapes the fees and delays associated with that process."

When do gifts of RLE make the most sense?

"There are two primary scenarios. The first is when the charity wants to use the land itself, for expanding a campus or building a camp for kids or something like that. The second involves land, which the charity doesn't want to use, but which is valuable and likely to become more valuable over time — real estate like farmland, property in the path of development or land in resort or vacation areas.

"In either situation, a gift of RLE allows the donor to retain use of the property while still ensuring it ends in the hands of the charity."

Source: Philip Purcell, Vice President for Planned Giving and Endowment Stewardship, Ball State University Foundation, Muncie, IN.
E-mail: ppurcell@bsu.edu

14. A Simple Way to Make Life Insurance Gifts Work for Your Cause

Looking for a way to promote life insurance as a viable giving option that makes sense for you and your donors? Ask donors to secure a new life insurance policy with your organization as the beneficiary, rather than asking them to sign over an existing policy.

This approach allows people of all income levels to significantly impact your organization by making small payments over time. The creation of a new policy also removes the potential risk of conflict with prospective heirs on an existing policy.

15. Make Life Income Gifts Work for Your Organization

Stewarding and cultivating donors for life income gifts can be a challenge, says Kenneth Wolfe, director, planned giving Programs, Colonial Williamsburg Foundation (Williamsburg, VA). But foundation officials have instituted several key strategies to ensure that their donors are aware of life income gifts and more willing to make them.

Wolfe says, "We subscribe to standard good administrative stewardship practices. If we steward the gift well, then the donor is more likely to contribute another life income gift to us." To do that, they:

- Recognize donors of life income gifts as members of the Legacy Society and invite them to an annual meeting held in Williamsburg each spring.

- Add life income donors to the foundation's mailing list to receive their donor magazine and the president's periodic update letter that goes to the foundation's closest friends and donors.

- Contact life income donors periodically (mail, telephone, personal visits) to update them on programs and activities (e.g., the things that their gifts will eventually support).

- Send a birthday card and a Colonial Williamsburg calendar each year.

Wolfe says the foundation's two most successful marketing initiatives for life income gifts are 1) full-page advertisements in their donor magazine, including a reply card bound into the magazine to make response easier, and 2) meetings between donors and development staff, including major gift officers. Wolfe says they have even had research staff visit planned giving donors when they are on the road attending conferences. "Thinking beyond your department silos is important, particularly in stewarding bequest donors."

Officials also do an annual special gift and estate planning presentation for top annual giving groups. Prior topics have included "Lessons from Benjamin Franklin's Will" and "Lessons from Famous Wills." They get some gifts as a result of their planned giving newsletter and information boxes on

their annual giving reply form, though not as many as they do from the advertisements and the one-on-one meetings.

Wolfe says the donor magazine is most helpful, because it solves one problem they have in reaching prospective life income donors. "Because we have an undefined constituency, we don't know a lot about our donors. The magazine goes to all of our donors. Therefore, the magazine ensures that the entire donor base gets this message in a cost-effective way. Additionally, it gets the message out consistently, which is important because the timing of these gifts is in the donor's control, not ours."

Source: Kenneth M. Wolfe, JD, CPA, Director, Planned Giving Programs, Colonial Williamsburg Foundation, Williamsburg, VA. E-mail: kwolfe@cwf.org

Content not available in this edition

16. Prioritize Uses for Unrestricted Bequests

What happens when your organization is surprised with a six-figure bequest that has no strings attached? Do you use it for general operations? Do you earmark it for your general endowment?

Create and prioritize a top-10 list of ways you would earmark unrestricted bequests. Then you will be prepared to use both expected and unexpected funds in the most thoughtful and prudent way. And by all means, avoid using bequests to underwrite general operations. Doing so sends the wrong message to those who might consider future bequests.

Beyond a top-10 list, be sure that you also have on hand a board-approved planned gifts policy addressing any number of issues related to marketing, establishing, accepting and stewarding planned gifts. Use the box, right, as a checklist to review or create such a gifts policy.

Planned Gifts Policies

A board-approved planned gifts policy should address issues, including but not limited to:

- Ethics Statement
- Definitions/Terminology
- Duties and Responsibilities
- Instrument Guidelines
- Establishment Procedures
- Gift Acceptance and Approval Procedures
- Gift Acknowledgment
- Recognition/Stewardship
- Confidentiality Information

17. Don't Overlook the Frugal In Pursuit of Major Gifts

Too often, we in the advancement profession tend to look only for persons who generate high incomes as viable gift prospects. What we often fail to do as rigorously is identify those who may not be obviously wealthy but are experts at saving and investing their resources.

The lifestyle of many American millionaires is surprisingly frugal. They buy their clothes on sale and off the rack. They drive unassuming vehicles. And on those special occasions when they do choose to dine out, they carefully scrutinize each item on the menu before ordering and on the bill before paying.

The lesson for advancement professionals? Make a concerted effort to pay closer attention to people's saving and spending habits. Your most frugal constituents may, in fact, be among your most viable major gift candidates.

18. Build a Network Of Estate Planning Professionals

Ever wish you had greater access to major donors and those who advise them? Why not build a professional network of your own?

For more than a decade, Pepperdine University's Center for Estate and Gift Planning has done just that with its Pepperdine Estate Planning Network (PEPNET), a dues-paying organization dedicated to connecting and developing estate planning professionals.

"We have estate planners, attorneys, CPAs, CLUs, financial planners, trust officers, even a few appraisers," Stephanie Buckley, center director, says of its 100-plus members.

The network centers on quarterly meetings featuring a range of charitable planning presentations. Overseen by center officials, the meetings provide networking opportunities, plus the chance to earn continuing education credit toward members' professional designation requirements. Members also receive publications, case studies and access to the center's planning experts and resources.

Maintaining such a program is not without tangible benefits. Buckley says that a number of significant gifts have come through PEPNET advisors, but stresses that her staff is glad to assist with any member's proposal, not just those directly benefiting Pepperdine.

"We like to say that there is no competition among lighthouses," she says. "If a gift helps Pepperdine, great. But if it helps someone else, that's great, too."

Source: Stephanie C. Buckley, Director, Center for Estate and Gift Planning, Pepperdine University, Malibu, CA. E-mail: stephanie.buckley@pepperdine.edu

19. Estate Notes Guarantee Pledges, Enable Recognition

Planned gifts are an attractive source of revenue, but they can be difficult to integrate into the structure of a capital campaign. Should revocable bequest expectancies be counted toward campaign goals? Should donors who have merely pledged support receive the same recognition as donors who have actually provided it?

These kinds of problems can tie development offices in knots but can easily be avoided with estate notes, a simple but often overlooked planned giving vehicle that can have far-reaching consequences.

An estate note is an irrevocable pledge against a donor's estate, binding the estate to commitments remaining unpaid at the end of a donor or survivor's lifetime. Donors are free to make payments (designated in writing) against the note during their lifetime, though they are under no obligation to do so. Estate notes can also be structured to be met by a trust.

Because estate notes supersede other planning instruments, donors can establish one without revising existing estate plans. And because estate notes are irrevocable, they allow bequests to be counted toward campaign goals, enabling the donor to receive immediate recognition and stewardship efforts.

The biggest downside for nonprofits is the risk that an estate will not be large enough to cover a donor's obligations. Because of this, as well as the fact that younger donors often wish to transfer all assets to a surviving spouse or younger children, estate notes are often most effective with older donors.

20. Seek Real Planned Gift Stories

How often do you see planned gift literature describing in technical terms a charitable gift annuity or a charitable remainder trust, followed by a brief fictitious example to explain how each planned gift works?

Instead of fiction, go for fact. Ask friends of your organization who've made such gifts if you may share their stories.

While some planned gift donors prefer anonymity, others will be willing to share the story of their gifts, if it helps encourage others to do the same.

Share as many details as possible. Tell how the gift is to be used, gift size, tax breaks realized as a result of the gift, the return the donor is receiving for the remainder of his/her life (and the life of his/her spouse), and more.

Each of these are valid sales tools, if you have donors ready and willing to share their stories. So ask them. Their willingness to help may surprise you.

21. Gifts From New Donors May Be Trial Balloons

Have you ever considered the possibility that some donors who send a first-time gift are simply testing you to determine whether your cause is worthy of a much larger gift? They may be floating a trial balloon to determine what sort of response their gift triggers.

It happens all the time, sometimes knowingly and other times unknowingly.

That's why it's important to respond professionally to all gifts and to consistently demonstrate good stewardship practices, regardless of gift size.

22. Seek Testimonials From Heirs of Planned Gift Donors

Here's a story idea for your upcoming planned gifts newsletter, constituency-wide newsletter or magazine:

Find children of planned gift donors who are willing to make positive comments about their parents' planned gift to your organization. Then build an article around their story.

What a positive message it would be for the son or daughter of a donor to say, to the effect: "I'm so glad my parents are doing more than leaving their entire estate to me. They've taught me some valuable lessons about life, and this is just another great example of what it means to be a responsible and caring human being. I intend to follow their example and make charitable provisions in my estate, as well."

Human-interest topics such as this will be more likely to be read by others, and provide a positive message to share with other planned gift prospects. Although it's necessary to communicate more technical information with planned gift prospects on your mailing list (e.g., tax benefits of particular planned gifts, descriptions of various planned gift vehicles), make a point to focus on the human element, as well.

23. Invite Planned Gift Donors to Make Board Testimonials

You'd think that asking members of nonprofit boards to make planned gifts would be like preaching to the choir. But ,in reality, many nonprofit boards don't set the example they should be expected to when it comes to making planned gifts. If this is the case in your nonprofit, you may want to invite a willing planned gift donor to attend a regular board meeting to explain what motivated him/her to make a planned gift.

In addition to motivating board members to make planned gifts, the presentation of a planned gift donor to your board is a wonderful way to recognize him/her and to formally say thank you.

You can be sure that those board members who elect to make a planned gift to your organization will be much more qualified to encourage others to consider establishing planned gifts as well.

Rule of Thumb

- Expectancies are planned gift commitments known to have been made to your charity but not yet realized because the donor is still living. As a guide only, you may assume that your charity is aware of one in six such expectancies in advance of receiving them. Example: If you know of 10 expectancies, there are probably at least 60 expectancies to be received at some point.

24. Build an Active, Accomplished Planned Gifts Committee

Many nonprofits take the time to form a planned gifts committee that meets occasionally but accomplishes little. That's a waste of everyone's time.

To build an active planned gifts committee, one whose members are really working to help promote and assist with planned gifts activities:

Make expectations clear. Develop a roles and responsibilities statement that sets forth both group and individual expectations for the members of your committee. Review those responsibilities with committee candidates prior to their appointments.

Assist your committee in setting yearly goals that include quantifiable objectives (e.g., to individually identify and meet with no fewer than 10 planned gift prospects throughout the year).

Schedule regular meetings that include individual assignments. In addition to reviewing and approving planned gift policies, ask your chair to assign specific tasks to members (e.g., contacting prospects, calling on attorneys, participating

Planned Gift Committees Should Include the Creative

Don't limit your planned gift advisory group to attorneys, trust officers, accountants and insurance representatives. Be sure to include less technical persons who might have creative marketing ideas to offer — public relations or sales specialists, for example.

Nontechnical individuals can help your group look for new and creative ways to market planned gifts and steward those who have already expressed interest in your programs.

in a planned gift seminar).

Give the committee members the recognition they deserve. Devote a page to this group on your website, including photos and brief biographies. List their names on planned gift letterhead and in your planned gifts newsletter. Publicly introduce them at estate planning seminars and other related events.

25. Resources for Financial Professionals Help Attract Planned Gifts

Is your organization looking to expand its pool of major donors or attract more planned gifts? Reaching out to agents of wealth might be just the ticket.

The American Institute for Cancer Research (Washington, D.C.) does that with a website called the Estate Planner's Corner (www. rrnew.com/aicr-advisor/). "We have a mailing list of 40,000 financial planners and estate attorneys, and we are basically trying to keep them up to date with changes in estate planning law coming out of Congress and the IRS," says Richard Ensminger, director of gift planning.

Central to the website is the Estate Planner's Toolbox, a suite of online resources that includes an Internet-based charitable giving tax service, customized gift planning illustrations, an online gift calculator, a gift planning advisors grid and up-to-date listings of applicable federal rates. Bequest and asset transfer information, needed for directing gifts to the institute, is also available.

Further resources include a quarterly newsletter for financial professionals and a monthly Planned Giving Update, as well as longer booklets and brochures for both clients and estate planning professionals.

Ensminger says the strategic objective is keeping the institute's name in front of individuals who might be considering planned gifts. "When donors go to their financial planner or estate attorney and say they are interested in leaving money to a charity, but don't have a particular preference, we hope our name will come up in that conversation."

The hope seems to be well-founded, for not infrequently does the institute receive exploratory calls from financial professionals. In fact, officials recently closed a major gift in which the donor told her attorney she wanted to fund cancer research, he gave her the name of three possible organizations, and she ended up choosing the institute.

For organizations reaching out to estate planners for the first time, Ensminger advises keeping information fresh and up-to-date, and always having staff available to answer fundraising professionals' questions.

Source: Richard Ensminger, Director of Gift Planning, American Institute for Cancer Research, Washington, D.C. E-mail: R.ensminger@AICR.org

Content not available in this edition

Content not available in this edition

How to (Tastefully) Plug Your Organization

Materials designed for estate planners' use must be accurate, professional, and free from undue bias or spin. Yet the ultimate goal is facilitating the donation of major gifts and bequests. So how is this balance to be maintained? How aggressively can/should nonprofits be in pushing their own agenda?

The American Institute for Cancer Research (Washington, D.C.) offers one forthright, yet tasteful, answer. The following text appears in the introduction to all its planned giving booklets and brochures:

"Please feel free to call the Gift Planning Office at any time. Our toll-free telephone number is 1-800-843-8114 or contact us by e-mail at gifts@aicr.org. And please ... if the opportunity presents itself, inform your clients about how a gift, trust or bequest to the American Institute for Cancer Research can help in the fight against cancer, while also enhancing their personal tax, investment, retirement and estate plans."

---

26. Follow Up on Possible Bequests

After the death of someone who you believe has included your charity in his/her estate plans, is it acceptable to contact the attorney and ask questions? Yes.

Some development professionals are hesitant to contact estate executors or attorneys, fearing they will be perceived as too meddlesome. However, it is perfectly acceptable to know the status of estates that involve your organization, and your inquiry signals that you're aware of the decedent's intentions.

Contact those representing the decedent as you approach the end of your fiscal year. Ask for a status report on matters such as probate, disposition of property, inventory of assets and anticipated disbursement dates.

If carried out professionally, these contacts can work to build rapport with estate representatives that can have a positive impact on your organization.

---

27. Share the Story: 'Life of a Planned Gift'

Looking for more effective and creative ways to market planned gifts? Why not share a pictorial journal of someone who made a planned gift or is in the process of making a planned gift?

Whether you produce a DVD or video that can be distributed, create a podcast on your website, do a two-page spread in your magazine or a combination of all of these, the goal is to visually profile one individual's planned gift from beginning to end.

Here are two ways it might work:

1. Consider those who have made planned gifts in the past or a deceased individual whose bequest made a significant impact on your organization. Is there someone for whom you have photos and past correspondence available? Could you use your records to create a time line and summarize events leading up to that planned gift? Perhaps you can provide background on the donor, a description of the type of planned gift the donor established, when the planned gift became a reality, photos of those who benefited from the gift or how it impacted your organization.

2. If your files don't include an interesting past example, approach a living donor and begin to document that person and his/her gift for use at a future date. This approach could yield a great illustration for the future.

---

28. Work to Identify, Confirm Planned Gift Expectancies

No matter how thorough your communications efforts, you may be unaware of individuals who have, on their own, made planned gift provisions that will one day benefit your organization.

Although some individuals choose not to share their charitable estate plans with you, being aware of such expectancies is undoubtedly helpful. Knowing a donor's wishes during his/her lifetime ensures that a planned gift will meet the desires of the donor as well as the needs of the recipient organization.

Take steps to encourage those among your constituency to inform you if they have made planned gift provisions. Publish a list of reasons for planned gift donors to confirm their plans with you.

Here is an example of such a list that you can edit to fit your organization's needs.

Please confirm your planned gift intentions with our office so that you...

1. Can receive the recognition and thanks you deserve.
2. Will be included in our Heritage Society.
3. Meet our staff and be assured your wishes will be fully honored.
4. Utilize staff expertise to choose the planned gift method that best meets your needs.
5. Verify that our organization is able to accept any special terms that may have been included in your gift.
6. May be informed of all tax advantages available based on your planned gift.
7. Make new friendships based on mutual goals shared with our charity.

29. Three Tips for Winning Over a Reluctant Spouse

So you have the gift in sight that will take your organization to the next level. There's just one problem — the reluctant spouse. Your donor is ready to write the check, but his or her spouse isn't convinced.

Lisa Grove, deputy director and director of development, Contemporary Art Museum St. Louis (St. Louis, MO), says that challenge isn't insurmountable. Using these tips may help you get the gift:

- **Meet with the spouse one-on-one.** As long as you get the go-ahead from the donor, this can open a fresh avenue of communication. The spouse may be more comfortable discussing reasons behind his or her reluctance, if the donor is not present. This meeting can also help you to build a relationship directly with this person who has such influence on your major donor prospect.

- **Structure the gift in recognition of the donor.** Consider using the gift as a naming opportunity to honor the donor's support of your organization. The spouse may appreciate the effort you're making in recognizing the donor's hard work.

- **Give the donor and his or her spouse some control.** Let them jointly make some decisions about how the gift will be used.

Once you secure the gift, make sure to thank the spouse individually for helping to make it happen.

Source: Lisa Grove, Deputy Director and Director of Development, Contemporary Art Museum St. Louis, St. Louis, MO. E-mail: lgrove@camstl.org

30. Starting From Scratch? Build a Planned Gifts Prospect List

If you're just getting started with a planned gifts program, a key first step is to build a database of qualified names.

While those persons on your mailing list who have reached retirement make obvious prospects, it's important to screen and rescreen your list. Likewise, age should not prevent someone from being added. After all, life insurance is one of the most affordable major gifts a young person can make.

As you review names to be added to your list, consider:

- Individuals or married couples with no apparent heirs. This characteristic, when combined with senior citizen status, represents obvious candidates for planned gifts.
- Those who have made consistent gifts to your

organization over a long period of time, regardless of gift size.

- Persons who have served as volunteers or board members or received awards from your organization in past years.
- Current and former longtime employees.
- Those who support many nonprofits in your community, as this proven level of philanthropy may qualify them as planned gift prospects.
- Agents of wealth: trust officers, attorneys, accountants, insurance agents and other financial planners. While these professionals may not make a planned gift themselves, they can be helpful in influencing others by virtue of association with your organization.

31. Advance Planned Giving With Simple, Impactful Phrase

Developing a robust planned giving program involves considerable strategizing and effort. Fortunately, one highly effective method for raising program awareness is also extremely simple. Add this tagline to e-mail signatures, business cards, letterhead, newsletters, websites and the like:

Please remember (your organization's name) in your will and trusts."

32. Nurture Attorney Ambassadors

Anyone with planned giving experience will tell you that having attorneys gong to bat on behalf of your organization is helpful.

But how do you get attorneys on board? After all, attorneys will generally say that ethics prevent them from encouraging clients to make estate plans for a specific nonprofit. And that's true. However, when clients are the ones bringing up the topic of charitable gifts — seeking their attorney's advice — it's in your nonprofit's best interest to have attorneys familiar with your cause and the many ways that you accept gifts.

Building a corps of attorney ambassadors is a long-term investment that requires building respect for both you and the institution you represent. With a system in place, you can set annual objectives that include adding and cultivating a minimum number of these professionals to your centers of influence list.

To build an attorney ambassador corps:

- Meet one-on-one with attorneys in your area to summarize your planned gift program and leave your business card. Stop by at least once a year to update them on your organization and examples of planned gifts you've received.

- Put those attorneys on your mailing list to receive your newsletter, magazine and planned gifts newsletter.

- Be sure your planned gifts advisory committee — and, if possible, board of trustees — include attorneys.

- Cultivate attorney relationships by including these professionals in estate planning workshops for your constituency. If you coordinate workshops in other communities, recruit attorneys from those locations to assist with your effort.

- When you come across a charitable gift article that would interest your attorney ambassadors, send them a copy of it along with a personal note.

- Host a reception or luncheon for your agents of wealth. Have your CEO and other board members on hand to thank them for their interest in your cause. Cite examples of how planned gifts benefit those you serve.

- When your agency realizes planned gifts, don't overlook the attorneys involved in the distribution of assets. They will be much more amiable when future opportunities present themselves, if they have had a previously pleasant relationship.

33. Don't Let Counting Sour Planned Gifts

 To what degree should donors be asked to substantiate planned gifts?

"Consider the perspective embedded in that question — that donors can't be trusted, that they can't be counted on, that the organization has to control the gift. When you take a step back, you realize that there's no value in sending those kinds of messages — for either the donor or the organization. Donors will describe their gift to you, often in far more detail than you ask for, but only in the context of fulfilling their own dreams and ambitions. If you come at them from a perspective of control, they will push back, and rightly so."

Source: Kevin Johnson, Principal, Retriever Development Counsel LLC, Portland, OR.
E-mail: kevin@retrieverdevelopment.com

34. Three Key Tips for Calling On Major Gift Prospects

A lot of the nervousness you may feel about making calls on major donor prospects may come from not feeling fully prepared to make the call.

These tips will help diminish any reluctance and add to your confidence level:

1. **Think through what you want to say.** You may even want to write down your pitch and read it out loud to see how it sounds.

2. **Write down a list of points you want to make during the call.** This will help you not only organize your thoughts, but also make sure that you don't forget to ask or tell the donor something important.

3. **Review background information.** Review the prospect's file and, if necessary, do some additional research, jotting down interests, connection to your organization, past giving history, etc. This will show the prospect that you're well-prepared, help you carry the conversation and tailor the call to that individual.

35. Define Planned Gift Club Membership Requirements

Whatever you call your planned gift society's or club's group, be sure to weigh the options for membership in this group. Don't limit membership to only one or two types of planned gifts.

Any of these gift options may make the donor worthy of membership in your planned gifts group:

- A bequest through a will or living trust
- A beneficiary designation of a retirement plan
- A beneficiary designation of a life insurance policy
- Outright gifts of life insurance policies
- Charitable gift annuities

- Charitable remainder trusts
- Retained life estates
- Testamentary charitable trusts
- Gifts that provide a perpetual income stream to your foundation
- The legal document or paperwork that effectuates the gift
- A signed membership form to your organization's legacy council
- An irrevocable bequest pledge form

36. Planning Guidebooks Add Value to Donor Magazine

One proven way to engage major donors is to provide them with tools to achieve other desired goals while supporting a worthy cause.

At Northwestern University Feinberg School of Medicine (Chicago, IL), development staff have produced a family-focused estate planning guidebook exploring ethical wills and methods for equitably distributing estate among children.

"Declining economic conditions shifted a lot of people's priorities away from charity and towards taking care of family first," says Joanna Riester, associate director of donor relations. "This booklet was chosen to show how people can take care of their loved ones and still further their ideals through charitable giving."

The guidebook is part of an ongoing series designed to augment the office's biannual donor magazine. Developed in collaboration with a third-party vendor, each booklet/magazine pairing shares a common theme and highlights a central topic such as a featured giving vehicle or timely piece of news.

While the booklets are distributed primarily to subscribers requesting further information, development staff use the booklets as well, Riester says, noting that the range of topics covered makes them a useful grab-and-go resource for development officers.

Much of the copy featured in the guidebooks is provided by the vendor but can be tailored to specific donor stories or university events, says Riester. And while the materials cost $5,000 to $10,000 per issue (both guidebooks and magazine), Riester says she believes this is money well spent.

"Our donors are extremely generous, and we owe it to them to provide quality advice and planning options," she says. "These materials provide enough interest and substance to keep them turning the page and taking our next call."

Content not available in this edition

Source: Joanna Riester, Associate Director of Donor Relations, Northwestern University, Feinberg School of Medicine Office of Development, Chicago, IL. E-mail: J-riester@northwestern.edu

Development staff at Northwest University's Feinberg School of Medicine (Chicago, IL) share this 14-page estate planning guidebook with major donors. See the book in its entirety at: http://www.feinberg.northwestern.edu/giving/pdfs/ FamilyFocused2010.pdf

37. In a Down Economy, Develop a System to Secure Planned Gifts

Integrating gift planning into your major giving program is one of the top strategies to successfully weather the current economic storm, says Holly McDonough, director of development-gift planning, Minnesota Medical Foundation (Minneapolis, MN).

A planned gift, McDonough explains, is a creative and flexible way for fundraising organizations to ask donors for major gifts. Gift planning creates a bridge for donors looking for opportunities to support your organization when their cash flow and asset base are diminished. This method of giving can open the door for a deeper donor relationship and a larger gift.

What Is a Planned Gift?

A planned gift is a charitable gift that has a guaranteed value slated for a later date. A donor can give planned gifts via:

✓ A bequest in one's will.
✓ Naming a charity organization in a retirement plan or an insurance policy.
✓ Charitable gift annuities.
✓ Retained life estate.
✓ Outright gifts of excess property.
✓ Bargain sales using real estate.
✓ Charitable lead trusts.
✓ Blended gifts.

How to Promote Planned Gifts:

Promoting gift planning can be as simple as incorporating information about these programs into existing advertising for your organization. Advertising techniques may include:

✓ Establishing direct mail or telemarketing programs that allow donors to self-identify as having planned gift assets.
✓ Educating your major gift officers. By sharing gift planning options, says McDonough, a gift officer may move a donor from a transactional gift to a transformational gift, allowing for a larger, more meaningful gift.
✓ Developing a relationship with gift planning experts. Many planned gifts carry with them complex legal ramifications. While these legalities should not deter gift officers, the gift officers should be able to call upon gift planning experts or property attorneys to assist with more complicated gifts.

Source: Holly McDonough, Director of Development-Gift Planning, Minnesota Medical Foundation at University of Minnesota, Minneapolis, MN. E-mail: h.mcdonough@mmf.umn.edu

Another Option: Blended Gifts

Do you have donors with outstanding pledges for major gifts? Offer them the option of a blended gift that provides a smaller outright or pledged gift now with a balance in the form of an estate gift, advises Holly McDonough, director of development-gift planning, Minnesota Medical Foundation (Minneapolis, MN). Revisit the gift when the market turns around and discuss converting the planned gift back to a lifetime gift.

This strategy may actually increase the final gift, as research shows a majority of donors who include a nonprofit in estate plans never change their plans. And for those who do, the majority of changes are to increase the size of the estate gift.

Learn to Think Like an Estate Planner

For many gift officers, estate planning is a fundraising option that may seem too foreign, complex or messy to pursue.

Karen Ciegler Hansen, attorney with Felhaber Larson Fenlon & Vogt (Minneapolis, MN), disagrees. She sees estate planning as a unique opportunity in this economic climate that can pay off quite well in the long run.

Hansen offers simple tips for the estate-planning novice:

1. **Listen.** Any good gift officer knows the importance of listening to a donor's hopes for his/her gift. With estate gifts, it is important to also listen to the donor's desires and concerns. Some common concerns for which to listen for are:

   ❑ **Concern for asset value.** Many estate holders worry their assets will be greatly diminished by the time they pass away. To ensure the estate holder leaves sufficient funds to his/her family, use a math formula in the estate plan. While an estate planning professional will have to work out the logistics, suggest a percentage gift rather than specific dollar amount, so the gift automatically adjusts with changes in the economy. It is also common practice to treat the receiving nonprofit as an additional child in the family.

   ❑ **Concern for how their inheritance will be used.** Many estate holders may have complex feelings about their heirs' relationship with money. They may feel that their children will not value the inheritance and will spend it inappropriately. In this case, you can advise donors that they can exemplify their own values to their children by leaving a certain percentage of their assets to charity.

   ❑ **Concern for their heirs' financial well-being.** On the opposite side of the coin, Hansen explains, many philanthropists have concerns that their children will never be financially self-sufficient, due to economic circumstances, disabilities or other issues. In this case, the donor may be open to the possibility of leaving money for his/her children in a trust during that child's lifetime, and mark the remainder for charity.

2. **Be flexible.** In tenuous economic times, clients want flexibility and fewer strings attached to planned gifts and estate plans. Write flexibility clauses into gift contracts, so estate holders feel free to adjust committed gifts at any time. This may also increase your odds of securing a gift)

3. **Collaborate.** Estate planners and other professional advisors can guide you through the estate-planning process while helping you to provide donors with the confidence that they have the information needed.

Source: Karen Ciegler Hansen, Attorney, Felhaber Larson Fenlon & Vogt, St. Paul, MN. E-mail: khansen@felhaber.com

---

38. Practice Your Presentation Delivery

Even if you're a veteran development pro, it doesn't hurt to hone your one-on-one presentation skills. These presentation exercises will help improve your delivery:

1. Write out a presentation summary. Doing so forces you to identify key messages you want to convey.

2. Use notecards to develop a presentation outline, then practice with and without them.

3. Go through your presentation, first with a colleague, then with someone less familiar with your nonprofit. Select someone who will give you honest feedback.

4. Prepare a list of possible questions and objections. Review each of them and develop convincing responses.

Although there is no substitute for the real thing, the more you plan and prepare for important presentations, the more convincing you will be to would-be donors.

39. Life Insurance Gifts Perfect for a Sluggish Economy

Does your organization accept gifts of life insurance? If not, it's missing out on a valuable revenue stream, says George Willock, director of the Office of Trusts, Estates and Gift Planning at Auburn University (Auburn, AL).

Willock notes that not only are these gifts irrevocable (unlike the majority of planned gifts), many donors continue giving current-dollar gifts in addition to an insurance policy. Moveover, he says gifts of life insurance are particularly attractive in tough economic times.

"With the economy like it is now, many people just aren't willing to part with money in current gifts. But someone who is reluctant to give $100,000 up front might very well be willing to pay $10,000 over five or ten years for a $100,000 policy."

What kinds of policies are best? Willock advises avoiding term insurance at all costs, as it gives the charity little control over the process. As soon as the donor stops paying premiums, there is no cash value left in the policy.

Instead, he recommends permanent policies that hold cash values through age 100, such as whole life, universal life and adjustable life. Variable universal and variable adjustable can also be used, provided the cash value equals the death benefit at age 100.

For organizations exploring life insurance for the first time, establishing a comprehensive set of gift acceptance policies is the number one priority, says Willock. Next, a supporter who is a knowledgeable agent should be asked to explain the basics of insurance operations. Finally, the donor base should be checked to see if any current supporters are licensed life insurance agents. The goal in this last step is to find agents with whom you can build rapport and who will comply with your gift acceptance policy.

The biggest mistake organizations make with life insurance programs? Allowing insurance agents or donors to dictate the terms of policies. "I've learned that a gift is not a gift unless it is accepted by the receiver," says Willock. "Just because someone wants to give a policy doesn't mean it is something the charity should accept. That's why having — and using — a really sound acceptance policy is so important."

One of the biggest challenges Willock says organizations will face with a new life insurance program is administering policies. "Making sure the premiums are paid, making sure donors get their contribution deductions, reviewing every policy every year — those things should be handled and controlled by the planned gifts office," he says. Though this work might require an additional staff position, Willock says that when Auburn's program started, it was not as overwhelming as some had feared.

Source: George Willock, Director, Office of Trusts, Estates and Gift Planning, Auburn University, Auburn, AL.
E-mail: willoge@auburn.edu

The Proper Care and Feeding Of Life Insurance Agents

Insurance agents are a key component of any life insurance fundraising strategy, so care should be taken in building mutually beneficial relationships with them, says Gerorge Willock, director of the Office of Trusts, Estates and Gift Planning at Auburn University (Auburn, AL).

"They should be allies," he says. "If a donor is late on a premium payment or is having trouble making payments, the first person you should call is the agent. It's their responsibility to see the donor and get the problem sorted out."

To start building a stable of agents, he suggests looking for donors or other supporters like alumni who are licensed agents, because they might be willing to suggest your organization to their clients. (He also suggests sticking with life insurance agents, as opposed to property or casualty agents who are not as familiar with the intricacies of life insurance policies.)

Establishing a strong agent network can have long-lasting and far-reaching consequences. "We've worked with maybe 150 agents over the past 10 years, and 20 to 25 have been very consistent in going to their client base and raising money on behalf of the university," says Willock. "They have become true volunteers who are constantly looking for opportunities for their clients to support us."

40. Convince Board Members to Make Planned Gifts

It's worth your investment of time to convince board members to make planned gifts to your organization.

Why, you ask? Several reasons:

1. If board members aren't sold on the value of planned gifts to your organization, how can they expect others to make such gifts?

2. Likewise, board members who have made planned gift provisions will be much better equipped to sell others on the idea.

3. Board members — more than any other constituency — should realize the tremendous good that can be accomplished through the realization of major planned gifts over time.

The more your board members own your planned gifts program, the more likely they are to set an example for others to follow.

Here are some strategies you can use to convince your board members to make planned gifts to your organization:

- Enlist assistance of existing planned gift donors to help sell your board.

- Use regular meetings to educate board members on various aspects of planned gifts — types of gifts, ways they can be directed, naming opportunities and so forth.

- If you have a planned gifts society, invite board members to help host its events.

- Use board meetings to recognize those who have made planned gifts.

- Ask individual board members to help in identifying planned gift prospects.

- List the names of your board on all planned gifts materials — brochures, letterhead, newsletters, etc.

- Get your board to own and endorse your planned gifts policies and procedures.

41. Trial Closing Techniques

As you work to close gifts with potential donors, ask an occasional question to measure the prospect's interest level:

- "What appeals to you more: helping financially deserving students get scholarship help or supporting our athletic program?"

- "How are we doing at this point?"

- "Does the idea of recognizing your parents appeal to you?"

- "How does the timing for such a gift fit with your circumstances?"

42. Ask the 'Passion Question'

Rather than telling your donors what fund to contribute to, ask the "passion question," suggests Lola Mauer, director of annual giving, University of South Carolina (Columbia, SC).

Ask your donors: "What is an area or program that you can support that would really mean a lot to you?"

Help donors identify their passions and connect those passions to your cause, and the gifts will follow.

Source: Lola Mauer, Director of Annual Giving, University of South Carolina, Columbia, SC. E-mail: lmauer@sc.edu

43. Consider Charitable Gift Annuity Advantages

Don't overlook the charitable gift annuity as a viable planned gift option this year. Here's why:

1. Recent retirees who may choose to switch some stocks into fixed income arrangements can minimize capital gains and receive deductions as well.

2. They can dip into principal without fear of running out of savings.

3. Annuity payments are partly tax free during a recipient's life expectancy.

4. Charitable deductions benefit donors, especially those planning a Roth IRA conversion this year.

5. Baby boomers can replenish retirement nest eggs depleted during the recession by arranging deferred payment gift annuities.

Source: The Estate Planner, American Institute for Cancer Research, Washington, D.C.

44. Smaller Planned Gifts Are OK, Too

So often when we think of planned gifts, we think of six-figure bequests or more. But wouldn't you welcome a steady stream of $20,000 or even $5,000 gifts each year?

Keep your sights on large planned gifts, but encourage planned gifts of any size, recognizing that a steady stream of smaller planned gifts can be just as helpful as the occasional large bequest.

Many constituents don't consider a charitable planned gift, because they think a smaller one won't be needed or appreciated. So they dismiss the idea and decide to limit their gifts to those while they are living.

To encourage people to consider a planned gift, regardless of size, take these steps:

❑ Include articles in your planned gifts newsletter that talk about how even smaller bequests can positively impact your organization and those you serve. Be specific.

❑ Give equal publicity to realized smaller planned gifts as you do larger ones.

❑ When meeting one-on-one with would-be donors, emphasize the importance of all planned gifts regardless of their size.

❑ Encourage life insurance and similar gifts that don't require large outlays of money but will one day provide a sizeable gift.

45. Secure a Challenge That Leverages Planned Gifts

Have you ever heard of a challenge gift as a way to encourage more planned gifts? Here's how that might work:

Approach a financially capable donor — someone who already recognizes the importance of your planned gift program — to establish a $250,000 outright gift to use as a challenge: Any donor who establishes an irrevocable planned gift of $25,000 or more in the current fiscal year will have $25,000 added to the named fund (by the challenger) he/she sets up.

That would mean that up to 10 individuals who make irrevocable planned gifts would immediately have $25,000 added to an endowment fund in their names. Then, after their lifetimes, their bequests would be added to their funds as well.

No challenge donor willing to step up to the plate? Here's another option: If you already have general endowment dollars not tied to a specific fund and are just part of your general endowment, earmark $25,000 per person to establish the named fund in honor of each planned gift donor.

What a motivator that would be — to have someone match your irrevocable planned gift so the named fund would begin immediately!

46. Three Practical Strategies for Promoting Bequests

Since bequests are the most popular form of planned giving, it makes sense to continually promote them to your constituency. Here are three varied strategies for keeping the topic of bequests before your public:

1. **During any type of public gathering, never miss an opportunity to invite those present to consider your charity in their estate plans.** Whether your invitation is subtle or direct, mentioning the topic says it's important to your organization's future. If appropriate, state, "If you have made provisions but not informed us, please do."

2. **Don't be shy about publicizing the realization of a bequest.** The more examples the public sees, the more they realize your organization must be worthy of such gifts. These examples also provide you with additional opportunities to broadcast key messages: "Our board of trustees has approved a policy whereby all undesignated bequests will be directed to our endowment, thus perpetuating the donor's generosity for generations to come."

3. **Identify persons who share their intentions to include your charity in their estate plans and are willing to assist in encouraging others to do the same.** Determine ways such persons can help you promote bequests — testimonials at public functions, profiles in your newsletter or magazine, accompanying you on planned gift visits — and make use of their example. Engaging such willing individuals in your planned gift program will make them feel even more committed to your cause.

47. Get Your Board Engaged In Backing Planned Gifts Programs

Your board's support (or lack of it) for your planned gifts program will impact its long-term success. Enthusiastic support can accelerate planned gifts tremendously.

Consider these steps to strengthen your board's commitment to and involvement in marketing planned gifts:

- Evaluate planned giving programs of nonprofits more advanced than yours and share findings with your board to raise your board's sights.

- Work with your board to establish planned gift goals. Engage members in shaping challenging yet realistic goals.

- Involve your board in establishing and evaluating a planned gifts policy. Does your nonprofit accept charitable remainder unitrusts? Should the board OK accepting bequests that include restrictions? Addressing such ongoing questions establishes the foundation of your planned gifts program and engages board members.

- Set a yearly calendar of activities and events inviting board participation: estate planning seminars, recognition of planned gift donors and more.

- Involve board members in shaping your planned giving budget. Share an itemized budget to show what you are able to accomplish plus what additional resources could do.

- Recognize board members who give time and support to your planned gifts efforts to keep them motivated and encourage others to become more involved.

- Meet one-on-one with board members to seek their input and expertise. Invite board members to make referrals and help in the cultivation of likely prospects.

- Invite individual board members to make planned gift commitments to your cause.

- Keep board members abreast of information affecting the world of planned giving: issues being addressed at the national level, demographics and more.

Establish Planned Gift Goals

Involve your board in establishing quantifiable objectives that move your program forward in securing new planned gifts. Consider goals such as:

- ❑ To identify ____ planned gift prospects in the current fiscal year.

- ❑ To average ____ personal visits each week with planned gift prospects.

- ❑ To solicit a minimum of ____ planned gifts throughout the current fiscal year.

- ❑ To secure ____ planned gift expectancies amounting to at least $____ during the current fiscal year.

- ❑ To expand the planned gifts mailing list by ____ during the current year.

- ❑ To conduct ____ estate planning seminars during the current year.

- ❑ To enlist ____ centers of influence who will assist our planned gifts efforts by identifying and cultivating would-be donors.

- ❑ To invite all board members to consider our charity in estate plans.

---

48. Suggest Residual Bequests as One Giving Option

As you cover the topic of charitable bequests with planned gift prospects, don't forget to suggest the residual bequest as one option.

Residual bequests are gifts of the remainder of an estate after all specific bequests have been distributed.

When combined with specific bequests, residual bequests allow the donor to ensure friends and relatives are adequately provided for, while still making a gift to charity.

Unrestricted Residual Bequest

I give (Name of Nonprofit, Address), (_____ percent of the residue of my estate) or (the sum of $_____) to be used by (Name of Nonprofit), wherever the needs and opportunities are greatest.

---

49. Advisory Council Focuses on Boosting Planned Gifts, Educating Community

Community Education Series Educates Public on Planned Giving

A major role the planned gift advisory council at Wentworth-Douglass Hospital & Health Foundation (Dover, NH) fulfills is educating the community about issues related to planned giving. One way the council accomplishes this is through its community education series.

Series offerings for 2011 focused on a variety of topics while engaging experts with a wide range of professional expertise, including:

- **"Charitable Planning: Doing Well by Doing Good"** with Bernie Lebs and Patrick F. Olearcek, JD, CLU, ChFC, MassMutual Financial Group

- **"The Economy and Markets – Score-card of 2010 Predictions and Top 10 Predictions for 2011"** with Jay Levy, Merrill Lynch & Jared Watson, BlackRock Private Investors

- **"How to "Do" Estate Planning With or Without the Federal Estate Tax"** with Bruce Johnson, Johnson & Associates & Tom Levasseur, The Beacon Retirement Group

- **"How to do more with what you have: Leveraging your Legacy"** with Robert Boulanger, Oppenheimer & Co., Inc. & Ken Money, Money Law Offices

- **"Veteran's Benefit"** with Rich Hilow, Financial Advisor, Edward Jones

- **"College Financial Planning"** with Melanie Dupuis, CPA, CCPS, Larry Raiche & Company CPAs

- **"Get the Facts"** A Reverse Mortgage Educational Event with Tom Torr, Cochecho Elder Law Associates & Kathleen Burke, Wells Fargo Home Mortgage

- **"Guardianship and Powers of Attorney—When Kids Become the Parents"** with Stephanie Burnham, Stephanie K. Burnham & Associates

- **"Re-Thinking Retirement Planning"** with Tom Levasseur, The Beacon Retirement Group & Karen Zaramba, Hunter Advisor Group, A Capital L member firm

- **"Saving Employee Benefit Costs While Keeping Employees Happy"** with Mark Jacobsohn, RELAYER Benefits Group, LLC

- **"Changes in Taxation Due to Current Political Environment that Impact Retirement, Investment and Planned Giving"** with Dave Verno, CPA, Leone, McDonnell & Roberts, PA

A planned gift advisory council is having a major impact on planned giving at Wentworth-Douglass Hospital & Health Foundation (Dover, NH).

According to Deborah Shelton, vice president of philanthropy & chief philanthropy officer, the foundation is slated to receive at least 50 new planned gifts, with approximately 100 donors participating in its planned giving program.

Shelton credits much of that activity to the advisory council that includes estate-planning attorneys, financial planners, benefit professionals, certified public accountants, trust officers and other allied professionals.

The council meets five times a year. Meetings begin with a half-hour open forum about the hospital, followed by a business meeting. Members are expected to assist in identifying and nurturing persons capable of making a planned gift to the foundation, support the foundation themselves through gifts to the annual appeal and attend planned meetings and workshops as their schedules permit.

The members also offer a community education series, educating the public on issues involved with planned giving (see box, left).

To further engage these valued professionals and make them feel invested in the hospital and health foundation, Shelton says, she and her staff invite them to all open houses and special events.

Source: Deborah Shelton, Vice President of Philanthropy & Chief Philanthropy Officer, Wentworth-Douglass Hospital & Health Foundation, Dover, NH. E-mail: Deborah.Shelton@wdhospital.com

Content not available in this edition

50. For Those Considering Restricted Bequests...

Encourage donors — especially those considering restricted planned gifts — to consult with your charity prior to making final estate planning decisions to help guarantee the gifts are used as they intended.

Anyone making a restricted planned gift unbeknownst to the charity runs the risk of: 1) the bequest being disqualified from the estate tax charitable deduction or 2) the charity rejecting the gift because of the nature of the restriction.

At the least, donors should consider a conditional bequest that would fail upon the occurrence or nonoccurrence of some event. A conditional bequest remains tax deductible if, at the time of the bequestor's death, the likelihood of the bequest failing is so remote as to be negligible.

51. Encourage Outright Gifts Along With Planned Gifts

There are those who have indicated they have included your charity in their estate plans but have never made a significant outright gift. And there are those who have done both. To encourage the first group to make an outright gift (in addition to a planned gift), ask those who have done both to provide testimonials about why they are gratified to have done so.

52. Encourage Constituents to Inform You of Charitable Plans

At nonprofits, it's common to discover the organization has been included in someone's estate plans after the donor's death.

While such bequests are welcome surprises, it is in the best interest of both the recipient and donor that charity officials be informed during the donor's lifetime — not after his/her death — of a planned gift intent. By confidentially informing staff of charitable plans in advance, the donor can be sure his/her gift will be used as intended and that it will be most effectively meeting the needs of the charity as well.

Advance knowledge of estate plans also enables nonprofit officials to recognize the donor during his/her lifetime (if so desired) and make the donor more aware of the charity's services and plans.

The charity's advance knowledge of a bequest, on the other hand, alerts officials to the likelihood of the eventual gift — to ensure proper cultivation happens — and provides time to learn of the donor's intended use of the gift.

To encourage donors to inform you of charitable plans while they are still alive:

- Establish a planned gifts club or society that recognizes those who have included your charity in their estate plans. Include an annual event to formally induct new members.

- Give donors the option of having their names listed as members of the planned gifts club — in your annual report, on a club plaque, etc. — on an annual basis. Tell them that doing so also encourages others to consider similar gifts.

- Point out in planned gifts newsletters and other materials the benefits of sharing such information in advance.

- Cite examples (from other charities) in which the nonprofit was uninformed and the bequest was not used to its best or fullest capacity because of lack of advance communication.

- Create a challenge gift to match new planned gifts established over a specified period of time. Knowing their bequests will be matched may encourage some to step forward and notify appropriate officials of their plans.

The more informed you are of existing planned gifts, the better you can steward these donors and recognize their generosity during their lifetimes.

---

53. Market Life Insurance as Affordable Major Gift

Obviously most donors can't make a $100,000 gift to your cause. Or can they?

A life insurance policy can create a major gift with a minimal investment.

Once the donor makes a charity the owner and beneficiary of his/her policy, the donor's annual premium payments — in the form of a gift to the charity — become tax deductible. Depending on the donor's age and the particular policy, he/she can make a $100,000 gift — the death benefit of the policy — for as little as $500 a year.

One of the best ways to learn firsthand how your charity can benefit from life insurance policies is to meet with a handful of insurance agents. Work to establish a collaborative effort in which they encourage prospects to consider establishing or turning over life insurance policies as a major charitable gift to your cause.

---

54. How to Develop a Planned Giving Marketing Plan

Before you launch your next marketing effort, make sure to include the four processes critical to the success of any marketing effort, says Ann McPherson, a marketing consultant with PG Calc (Cambridge, MA).

Specifically, McPherson says, your marketing effort plan should: 1) establish and articulate objectives; 2) define the strategy; 3) execute the tactics of the program within the budget; and 4) measure, report and refine.

"These four processes should be applied to both your annual plans and individual marketing initiatives," McPherson says. "They operate sequentially and are dependent on one another."

Here, McPherson further defines the four critical elements:

1. **Establish and articulate objectives.** Select both tangible, measurable goals that you can realistically achieve, and less quantifiable goals; she says: "Well-defined objectives allow marketers to articulate clearly and succinctly what the marketing program seeks to achieve; making the objectives measurable allows them to demonstrate success when it happens — or learn valuable lessons if the result is less successful than forecasted. Regardless of your specific objectives, one of the most important activities you'll need to engage in if your program is going to succeed is a consideration of organizational support, both external and internal. By establishing enthusiasm for your efforts, you'll ensure you have continued support to see it through to your projected outcomes."

2. **Define the strategy.** Conducting a SWOT analysis (Strengths, Weaknesses, Opportunities, Threats) of your organization's mission will help you draft a precise, carefully crafted value proposition, position your organization relative to its competitors and peers, and develop a deep understanding of the target audiences to use as leverage in the marketing process; she says: "Your target audiences may be varied and each segment requires different messaging, as well as different frequency of communications and information. Target audiences for most planned giving officers include long-term annual fund donors and major gift donors, as they have indicated a certain charity as being of particular interest to them; communities of advisors, as they have proven to be influential when it comes to their clients' charitable intent; and existing planned gift donors, who are often likely to make a repeat gift arrangement."

3. **Execute the tactics of the program within the budget.** If a program's objectives have been well defined and the strategic planning diligently conducted, the executive phase should proceed smoothly, she says. One way to help you execute the tactics of the program within the budget is to build a spreadsheet listing the various activities that will help you accomplish your objectives and the dates associated with their development and implementation, says McPherson. "A spreadsheet can help you manage each task and provide all of your team members with a visual summary of their responsibilities. Typical data captured include 1) elapsed time for tasks, 2) the number of hours associated with each task, 3) the cost associated with each deliverable and 4) ownership for each task. The process of building the spreadsheet is valuable in itself since it requires a marketer to spell out every step required in the execution of the program and indicates dependencies."

4. **Measure, report, refine.** Because of lengthy cultivation cycles, assigning dollars raised to any particular campaign may be impossible; she says: "Recognize, instead, that each campaign you pursue produces some success even if it's hard to measure. This does not mean that you should stop measuring. Rather, it is better to keep paying attention to best practices; reviewing, documenting and improving upon internal benchmarks; and most importantly, talking to donors and prospects about their thoughts on communications they receive from your organization."

Source: Ann McPherson, Marketing Consultant, PG Calc, Cambridge, MA. E-mail: amcpherson@pgcalc.com

55. Five Rules for Preserving Planned Gift Expectancies

It's a major accomplishment every time you learn of someone who has included your organization in his/her estate plans since many donors choose not to share that information during their lifetimes. But once you're aware of an expectancy, what are you doing to maintain or even solidify the relationship?

Adapt these five precepts to help ensure the donor won't reverse his/her estate plans:

1. **Get a good reading on what matters most to the individual.** Understanding donors' personalities and motivations for giving will help determine the level of attention and/or anonymity they receive.

2. **Practice good stewardship even if it may be years before you realize the gift.** A young person who makes a commitment to contribute a life insurance policy, for instance, deserves the same attention as a senior citizen who has made a bequest.

3. **Have programs in place that recognize those who choose to be recognized.** While not everyone desires attention, develop programs that recognize those who do appreciate recognition — a heritage society with accompanying benefits, listings in your annual report and on a plaque in a public location of your facility, etc. Such programs let the public know you're in the business of accepting planned gifts.

4. **Keep the communication regular but varied in the method of delivery.** In addition to broad-brush cultivation efforts — a quarterly planned gift newsletter, a general newsletter or magazine, invitations to events, etc. — provide individual communications such as face-to-face meetings, personal correspondence and lunch with your CEO that keep these important persons involved and in the know.

5. **Honor donors' confidentiality.** Planned gifts are a very personal matter. Print "in strictest confidence" on planned gift communications and stress your high level of confidentiality whenever discussing planned gift matters.

56. Connect With Your Community's Native Sons and Daughters

Based on the type of nonprofit you represent — your mission, programs and services — could you justify a program intended to connect with former residents of your community, people who were born or grew up there but now live elsewhere?

Find sincere ways to connect with native sons and daughters and there's no limit on what you can do by cultivating relationships with financially capable individuals who are part of this group.

Here are some examples of how you might cultivate relationships with your city's or state's natives:

1. **Start a Who's Who of your city or service region.** Work at building a list of natives who have gone on to achieve success and any degree of celebrity. This becomes your working list of those to be approached and cultivated. Talk to old-timers who can help identify those persons. Visit with the alumni offices of your city's colleges, universities and schools to identify their Who's Who lists. Talk to chamber of commerce officials to see if such a list already exists in their office. You may even decide to form a Who's Who advisory committee to help with this undertaking.

2. **Identify ways to reconnect natives with their hometown (or state).** Share news clippings, historical accounts and more. Involve old friends and relatives to help re-establish ties and make introductions with your organization.

3. **Take the lead in establishing a yearly event that invites former residents back.** If a community festival of some sort already exists, use that as a homecoming connecting point.

4. **Initiate an annual awards program that selects community natives based on their achievements.** You may choose to collaborate with your local chamber or other organizations to make this program more encompassing.

5. **Build a Web page geared to your community's native sons and daughters.** Share your Who's Who list on the site and include brief biographies on each or limit them to past awards recipients. Include links to your community's history and points of interest. Offer trivia questions about your community to which visitors can respond. Include a gallery of former residents' photos.

57. Suggest Deferred Payment Gift Annuity to Younger Crowd

Your younger planned gift prospects — say, those persons ages 40 to 60 — may wish to consider a deferred payment gift annuity as a planned gift option, especially if they have a high income, need to benefit now from a current tax deduction and wish to add to future retirement income.

The deferred payment gift annuity involves the current transfer of cash or marketable securities, in exchange for which the nonprofit agrees to pay the donor an annuity starting at some future date (at least one year after the date of the gift). The gift can consist of a single transfer, a series of transfers or periodic transfers to the plan in high income years.

The donor realizes an immediate charitable deduction for the gift portion of each transfer to the deferred gift annuity plan. A portion of each annuity payment, when the payments begin, will be a tax-free return of principal over the life expectancy of the annuitant.

When appreciated long-term capital gain securities are transferred, any reportable capital gain is spread over the donor-annuitant's life expectancy.

A deferred payment gift annuity may be established for the benefit of one or two individual annuitants, and the donor need not be one.

Deferred Payment Gift Annuity Features, Benefits

- Donors receive payments at least annually once they begin.
- Donor's fixed-dollar income is guaranteed for life.
- Income is based on age of the beneficiaries and length of deferment until payments begin.
- A charitable deduction is allowed immediately for the present value of donor's gift.
- A portion of the income is tax-free over the expected life of the gift annuity.
- The donor benefits from favorable capital gains treatment and deferral of capital gains until the date the annuity begins if the annuity is funded with appreciated assets.
- Deferred payment gift annuities help reduce the donor's estate tax and probate costs.

58. When Planned Gift Prospects Live Far Away

Do you have planned gift prospects who live far from your institution or agency? Most organizations do — alumni, former residents of a community, chapter members and others.

Whether such individuals have confirmed their intent to include your charity in their estate plans or it is possible that they will do so at some time, how do you cultivate a relationship and maintain their interest from such a distance?

Here are some strategies for stewarding long-distance planned gift prospects:

Establish a tickler system. Send regular messages from your institution at irregular intervals. Create a monthly reminder of who should receive a phone call, a birthday or anniversary card, or other appropriate (not contrived) communication.

Send a videotape. Produce a once-a-year video — using an inexpensive camcorder to keep expenses down, if necessary — that can be distributed to all faraway prospects. Provide a narrated tour of your facility; interview some employees or those served by your organization; or produce a nostalgic "I Remember When" video for older prospects.

Send there's-no-place-like-home reminders. For former residents of your area, send reminders of their hometown links — products produced in your community/state, books/periodicals with regional flavor or news clippings from your local newspaper.

Include personal notes with each planned gifts newsletter. If you produce a quarterly planned gifts newsletter, include an occasional personal note for some of your faraway clients to personalize the mailing.

59. How to Best Market Your Planned Giving Program

Good marketing is crucial to an effective planned giving program. Alison O'Carroll, senior consultant at PG Calc (Seattle, WA) has seen firsthand just how important it can be.

"An organization I worked with had a planned giving program that was raising about $3 million a year," she says. "Senior leadership decided the program was so strong that its marketing budget could be eliminated. Within three years, planned gift revenue had dropped to under $1 million a year."

Carroll shares a wealth of experienced-tested tips on effectively marketing your planned giving program.

What's the first thing people should know about marketing planned giving?

"When it comes to planned giving there are two kinds of marketing — internal and external — and internal is just as important as external. People's thoughts often go straight to direct mail, but you really need to start by selling the program to your staff, leadership and board. This builds support and avoids the go-all-in or drop-it-completely extremes that sometimes afflict planned giving. Internal sources can also be a great source of referrals. Many organizations get over half their planned giving leads internally."

"Internal (marketing) is just as important as external ... you really need to start by selling the program to your staff, leadership and board."

How is marketing planned giving (externally) different than marketing other kinds of fundraising?

"Planned giving depends on the donor's lifecycle more than other kinds of fundraising. Just like tires are on sale every week, but you never notice until you need a tire, the success of a planned giving message depends on the donor being in a frame of mind to receive it. It's a message that needs to be there when it's right for them — at retirement, when a child graduates, after a death in the family — so it needs to be communicated as frequently and consistently as possible. To do that in a cost-effective way, you want to piggyback as much as possible on promotional materials already in use."

What might this piggybacking on other materials look like?

"Your newsletter should have space for planned giving — ideally in every issue. It could be a small mention, a one-page donor story or even a several-page feature. An e-newsletter could have a brief blurb — something like, 'Consider joining our legacy society. Contact Suzie Smith for more information.' Some organizations include planned giving inserts in acknowledgment letters — not asking for a planned gift, because you don't want to be tacky, but more of a 'Did you know you can make a gift in this way?' type of message. Inserts like that can also be included in annual fund mailers.

"The success of a planned giving message depends on the donor being in a frame of mind to receive it. It's a message that needs to be there when it's right for them."

"The packet you take on solicitation calls should include something on planned giving. You might want to consider putting materials on tables or at check-ins for special events. You could put estate plan taglines on e-mail signatures, stationery and envelopes. If you have a phone system where the caller hears a message while they wait, you could put an eight- to 10-second blurb on planned giving. And, of course, you want to put planned giving messages on your website. Basically, you want to use as many ways to get information out as you can."

What kinds of people make the best planned giving prospects?

"Bequests are the largest kind of planned giving by far, and asking people to put you in their estate plan next to their family and friends is a highly personal thing. So the best planned giving prospects are people you know well and who have demonstrated passion and loyalty for your organization. This would start with your board and

(Continued on pg. 31)

(Continued from pg. 30)

volunteer groups, but can also include advisory boards, emeriti boards, guilds, alumni advisory groups, and staff or faculty members, either current or retired. You'd be surprised how many organizations don't take advantage of their closest supporters."

What about direct mailings? What role do they have in planned giving?

"Mass mailings of 10,000 to 20,000 pieces are crucial to long-term success. Two mailings like that a year is good, three or four is even better. Some organizations do as many as seven or eight.

"To make the most of your mailing, you should also consider making follow-up phone calls. Even if you just pick recipients at random, the mailing created a reason to contact the donor..."

"You want to cover different types of giving like trusts and annuities, but you want at least half of your materials to focus on bequests. You should use a variety of materials like letters, tri-fold self-mailers, postcards and fliers. Testing will help you understand what achieves the best results, but it's also important to just vary things over time. One organization I worked with saw its response more than double when it switched to a new postcard format, but by the third postcard, response rates were back to what they had been previously. So change for its own sake can often be effective."

What kind of response is reasonable to expect from planned giving mailings?

"Response rates will be low — half a percent would be very good. But the handful of leads you generate are not the first purpose of the mailing. You need to start thinking in terms of educating your donor base. To make the most of your mailing, you should also consider making follow-up phone calls. Even if you just pick recipients at random, the mailing created a reason to contact the donor, and the call will increase the campaign's effectiveness."

What about planned giving messaging? How can it be improved?

"Keep your message very simple. Pick one main message and don't try to add too much to it. Planned giving material has a tendency to get overly technical, but you should fight that. Avoid the jargon we all use and stress the notion of legacy, the impact the gift will have."

Are there any new or novel approaches to marketing planned giving?

"In the past, telemarketing was just for annual funding, but more and more we're seeing it with planned giving as well. The idea makes some people nervous — planned giving seems a little too personal to be discussing over the phone — but we've seen very little pushback from donors. Outside vendors with calling programs are one way to go, but organizations with sufficient in-house callers can be successful at uncovering gifts and generating leads. You can also think about adding a few planned giving questions at the end of annual fund calls. It's not as effective as a stand-alone call, but it's better than nothing."

"Think about adding a few planned giving questions at the end of annual fund calls. It's not as effective as a stand-alone call, but it's better than nothing."

What metrics can be used to track the effectiveness of planned giving marketing?

"Planned giving has such a long time horizon, it's hard to measure success by dollars alone. One figure you want to track is the number of people who have put the organization in their will — the known bequests as I call them. You also want to capture why people respond to planned giving messaging, and from what channels they are responding. (Tracking that can be as simple as having gift officers ask.) Comparing the average annual gift size with the average bequest gift size is also a useful way to justify a planned giving program."

Source: Alison O'Carroll, Senior Consultant, PG Calc, Seattle, WA. E-mail: aocarroll@pgcalc.com

60. Look for Clues and Signals From Donors

Be on the lookout for clues and signals from annual gift donors who may want to do more and include your organization in their estate plans. Look for these three signals:

1. **Those who are always there.** Look for those people who always show up at events — those friends and supporters who keep coming to every event you host. Those are people to whom you need to pay attention.

2. **Those who pay you a visit.** The people who come into your facility or office when they don't have to may be trying to tell you something. They may be seeking your attention for any number of reasons.

3. **Donors who include personal notes with gifts.** Notes that are included with their annual gift could be a clue that these donors want to do more. They're giving you signals that they're interested in your organization and may want to explore additional ways of investing in your cause.

61. Incorporate Planned Giving Into Capital Campaigns

Planned gifts can be a source of great revenue and are being pursued in a wider and wider variety of contexts. While nonprofits often talk about incorporating planned giving into their campaign goals, very few actually do so with any degree of success, says Kevin Johnson, principal of Retriever Development Counsel (Portland, OR).

Part of the challenge is the difference of purpose between legacy and capital gifts, says Johnson. "The biggest value of a capital campaign is its single-minded focus. That's also the biggest obstacle to legacy giving," he says. "The sooner-is-better, cash-based mindset of a capital campaign is exactly the opposite of what is needed with legacy giving."

But the differences between the two don't mean they can't complement each other. Johnson offers the following suggestions for successfully incorporating planned giving into capital campaigns.

1. **Start a planned giving campaign before your capital campaign.** Planned gifts are often pursued in the waning months of a capital campaign, which Johnson thinks is the worst possible time. "Legacy gifts involve conversations about values and vision. Those are conversations you want to have before you approach someone in a capital campaign. If you've already established a match in values, the question donors will be asking won't be whether to give in support of capital projects, but how much to give."

2. **Watch the language used in soliciting legacy gifts.** When planned giving is mentioned in capital campaign solicitations, the language used often makes it seem like a secondary or optional gift, says Johnson. "Gift officers need to make sure legacy giving doesn't feel like a second-class conversation to donors," he says. "You definitely need to avoid any sense of, 'Gee, since you're too much of a loser to give a big gift now, how about a planned gift in the future?'"

3. **Relate legacy giving to immediate capital needs.** Giving legacy conversations as much weight as cash conversations is difficult if planned giving is not directly related to campaign goals, says Johnson. Making these concrete and tangible connections — providing funded depreciation for a building under construction, for example, or establishing an endowment to pay a program's future staff — will increase the likelihood of receiving planned gifts, he says.

4. **Keep systems of counting gifts clear — and separate.** "Counting gifts for the balance sheet is different from counting gifts for fundraising objectives, and mixing the two almost always does a disservice to the organization," says Johnson. "You should be tracking whatever metrics are most relevant to the fundraising goals you've adopted. Don't let the auditing/accounting conversation be your only source of metrics."

5. **Keep things (including terminology) simple.** The phrase "planned gifts" has, in Johnson's opinion, come to represent a set of dauntingly complex giving instruments in donors' minds. Because of this — and because 90 to 95 percent of all planned gift dollars come from simple bequests — he prefers the term "legacy giving"to planned giving. He also advocates framing donor expectations by focusing on the impact and values of gifts, rather than the mechanics of realizing them.

Source: Kevin Johnson, Principal, Retriever Development Counsel, LLC, Portland, OR. E-mail: kevin@retrieverdevelopment.com

62. Soliciting Life Insurance Gifts

Accepting gifts of life insurance policies can be lucrative, but it can also be problematic, depending on how the gift is made, says Adam Aptowitzer, a lawyer with Drache Aptowitzer (Ottawa, Ontario, Canada).

"If the individual names the charity as beneficiary, that is easy, and the nonprofit typically doesn't know about the gift until the donor's death," Aptowitzer says. But if the person donates a policy while he/she is living, the nonprofit must deal with the premium, he says. "If the nonprofit can't pay the premium, the donation might be worthless, although the nonprofit could secure a donation of the premium until the donor dies."

A major advantage of life insurance policies as gifts, he says, is that they can have a large payout for a small investment.

One disadvantage, says Aptowitzer, is the potential risk to a nonprofit's reputation related to accepting such gifts from donors who may later realize they still need the policy (and may be uninsurable by then), or there are dependents left with no means of support other than those donated policies.

Paula Straub, president, Save Gains Tax LLC (San Marcos, CA), former investment advisor representative and current insurance agent, agrees that in the right circumstances, gifts of life insurance policies can be advantageous for nonprofits. However, she says, in today's cash-strapped nonprofit environment, large monthly premiums can strain a nonprofit's resources.

Alternatives to turning away a gift based on inability to pay the premium are to ask the donor to sell the policy to a life settlement company and donate cash proceeds to the nonprofit, or for the nonprofit to accept the gift and sell it to a life settlement company itself, says Straub.

Here is a sampling of life settlement companies:
- The Life Settlement Company of America (www.lscoa.com)
- IMS Associates (www.ims-associates.com)
- Legacy Benefits (www.legacybenefits.com)
- Integrity Capital Partners (www.integrityp.com)
- Life Policy Group (www.lifepolicygroup.com)

Sources: Adam Aptowitzer, Lawyer, Drache Aptowitzer, Ottawa, Ontario, Canada. E-mail: adamapt@drache.ca
Paula Straub, President, Save Gains Tax LLC, San Marcos, CA. E-mail: savegainstax@gmail.com

63. Are You Ready for CGAs?

Charitable gift annuities (CGAs) — binding financial agreements between a nonprofit and a major donor — can be a great way to acquire large-scale donations. Yet, only a small percentage of nonprofits in the United States offer CGAs to major donors because of the planning and paperwork involved.

How do you know if your nonprofit is prepared to take on the added risk, responsibility — and reward — CGAs bring?

S.C. Chase Adams, managing director of Adams Associates (Ft. Lauderdale, FL), a law firm specializing in fundraising and estate preservation strategies, suggests referencing your organization's strengths and weaknesses against this five-point checklist:

1. **Are your books impeccable?** In a CGA with a donor, your organization is legally responsible for investing the donor's money in such a way as to guarantee payments to the donor, possibly for decades, requiring extra — and precise — accounting.

2. **How solid is your organization's long-term outlook?** With CGAs, nonprofits receive full ownership of the gift upon the donor's death. This is, of course, not something you can plan for, so the rest of your organization's long-term prospects need to be strong in the interim.

3. **What staff resources can you allocate or increase for the sake of CGAs?** The time, energy and expense of administering a CGA program can be onerous and expensive, says Adams. Tasks include record-keeping for each CGA account and completing a lengthy registration process each state requires before a nonprofit can enter into CGAs.

4. **What assets do you already have?** In some states, a nonprofit must pledge a percentage of assets as collateral to insure the donor's payments. Other states require that a nonprofit pledge all of its assets to qualify for CGA status.

5. **How much can you afford to financially invest in administering CGAs?** Although the adage usually applies to the for-profit sector, spending money to make money definitely applies to any nonprofit organization seeking CGAs.

Source: S.C. Chase Adams, Managing Director, Adams Associates, Fort Lauderdale, FL. E-mail: info@chaseadams.net

64. Offer Sample Bequest Wording

To realize more charitable bequests, it's important that your organization show constituents just how easy it is to make a bequest.

Offer sample bequest wording from time to time in planned gift literature, in your regularly published newsletter or magazine, on your website and in other appropriate communications. Also, be sure to point out the benefits to the donor of leaving a bequest to your organization.

To the right is an example of bequest wording.

> **Remember (Name of Your Organization) In Your Estate Plans**
>
> I, (full name) give, devise and bequeath to (Name of Your Charity), a (State) charitable corporation located in (City, State), the sum of $_____ (or: _____ percent of the residue of my estate and or other personal property appropriately described) to be used for _____ (or: to be used as its Board of Trustees shall deem advisable to best promote (Name of Your Organization's) objectives).

65. Follow Up Visits With a Summary Letter

Each face-to-face visit you have with a planned gift prospect is important. You will no doubt have some objective in mind each time you meet with a prospect — introduction, cultivation, solicitation or stewardship.

Following each visit, it's important to send a letter summarizing your meeting, especially since many aspects of planned gifts can be more technical and unique to the type of gift being considered, e.g., the gift amount, the age of the donor(s) and more.

A follow-up letter allows you to reiterate key discussion points and suggest next steps in formalizing a planned gift. Such a letter also helps to reflect a higher level of professionalism.

The generic letter shown here illustrates how a follow-up letter might read depending on the nature of your visit, what's being discussed and the unique characteristics of the individual with whom you are meeting.

XYZ Nonprofit

Dear Frank:

As always, it was a pleasure to have met with you this past week. I always enjoy our visits and have such great respect for you.

I thought it might be helpful to summarize our conversation as you consider the benefits of establishing a charitable gift annuity for XYZ Nonprofit.

Based on your age of 70, you could establish a charitable gift annuity that pays an annuity rate of 6.5 percent. In exchange for a cash gift of $10,000, XYZ Nonprofit will provide you with an annuity of $650 per year for the remainder of your lifetime. Of that $650, $280.15 will be treated as ordinary income and the remaining $369.85 as tax-free income (until year 2021). In addition, you can claim a current federal charitable income tax deduction of $4,118.47.

Also as we discussed, instead of using cash to fund your gift annuity, you could fund it with appreciated stock and receive additional tax benefits. By funding the gift annuity with stock that has appreciated in value and that has been owned for longer than one year, you would significantly reduce the federal and state capital gains taxes that would be incurred if you sell the stock yourself.

I'm assuming you may have additional questions about this type of gift so I'll plan to get in touch in a couple of weeks to set another time for us to get together and chat more about it.

Thanks again, Frank, for meeting with me and weighing the benefits — to you and to XYZ Nonprofit — of establishing a charitable gift annuity.

Sincerely,

Robert Griffin
Planned Gifts Director

---

66. Why a Quarterly Newsletter Makes Sense

Whether you produce it on your own or outsource the job through a planned gifts consultant, distributing a quarterly planned gifts newsletter makes good sense. Here's why:

- **It helps to position your organization in the minds of would-be donors.** There are plenty of nonprofit organizations vying for planned gifts. The absence of ongoing planned gift messages will result in missed opportunities.
- **It allows you to educate would-be and existing donors.** A periodic newsletter enables you to provide constituents with technical information about various types of planned gifts and the benefits of each.
- **It supplements your efforts to build relationships.** Personal visits, phone calls, events and more all help to nurture relationships that will either result in planned gifts or help to solidify existing gifts.
- **It can be used to inspire others and recognize donors' generosity.** A planned gifts newsletter enables you to recognize planned gift donors and underscore the impact of gifts that have been realized.

67. Identify Planned Giving Prospects Among Your Donor Base

Donors who currently give to your organization's annual fund or have made gifts to your capital campaign are great prospects for planned gifts. Your donor database has a wealth of information about current donors. That information is filled with clues about which donors may be great candidates for planned gifts. Here's what to consider:

- Women using Miss as a title — a possible indication that they're older and have no heirs.
- Those whose address indicates they have moved to a retirement community.
- Donors who have recently given multiple memorial gifts.
- Donors who have given over a period of 10 years or more, regardless of gift size.

- Alumni donors whose children or grandchildren also attended your school.
- Middle-aged (or older) donors who have no children.
- Those who have served as board members, advisory board members or volunteers.
- Those exploring gift options for their heirs (children and/ or grandchildren). Many planned giving vehicles can help these donors continue to provide for their heirs.

Here's another great way to identify planned giving prospects among your donor base: Profile your existing planned giving donors, looking for similarities in gender, type of planned gift made, age range, number of years giving and geographical location, then search your database for donors who fit those parameters.

68. Encourage Employees to Make Planned Gifts

Do you know who, among your employees, has no immediate heirs?

Most charities have individuals who are committed employees with no obvious heirs. And even if they do have heirs, they may be open to the idea of making a planned gift. It doesn't matter whether those persons are making large gifts or even smaller annual gifts to your organization. It does matter, however, that you recognize their ability to make a lasting planned gift to the organization they so dearly love.

To help encourage former and current employees to consider making a planned gift:

1. Involve them as volunteers in any capacity in your planned gifts program: helping with heritage society events, writing for your planned gifts newsletter, helping host an estate planning seminar and more.

2. Begin to explore planned gift opportunities that could positively impact those programs or services that matter most to them as employees.

3. Publicize and/or share examples of planned gifts from your organization — or other charities — that were made possible by employees.

4. Include at least one employee on your planned gifts committee or advisory council.

69. Estate Gift Predictive Model Increases Efficiency, Allows Age-targeted Marketing

Frank Robertson, director of planned giving at the University of Minnesota Foundation (Minneapolis, MN), can trace the birth of the foundation's estate gift predictive model to a single incident:

"A single woman, never married and no heirs, made small annual gifts for decades, but was never identified as a major gift prospect and was never personally contacted. No one knew this woman, but she ended up leaving the university more than $3 million. The potential lost in that relationship was what really prompted us to start looking for a more reliable way of identifying potential estate donors."

The predictive model developed by foundation staff uses factors common to many estate gift donors to rate a prospect's likelihood of leaving a gift to the university (e.g., consistency of annual giving, lack of children, marital status).

Robertson says the approach has allowed the foundation to more effectively identify potential donors while extending fundraising efforts to younger demographics without wasting resources. He offers two examples of how the model has facilitated a focus on younger prospects:

1. **Targeted newsletters**. The foundation maintains two versions of a fundraising newsletter. The younger version had been targeted at donors aged 55 to 64 (the older at 65-plus). With the estate gift predictive model, though, the floor was dropped to 40 and distribution was limited to likely donors. The result, Robertson says, was fewer copies being sent, but more people likely to give being reached, and at an earlier point in life.

2. **Will survey** (shown at right). Collegiate units of the university send periodic surveys (see sidebar below) seeking confirmation of estate gift commitments to the university. The first year the foundation dropped the minimum age of recipient from 65 to 40 and contacted only the top two designations of the predictive model (the very likely and likely to give categories), they posted a 4.1 percent response rate and received seven new estate commitments from donors under age 65.

Source: Frank Robertson, Director of Planned Giving, University of Minnesota Foundation, McNamara Alumni Center, Minneapolis, MN. E-mail: Rober038@umn.edu

Will Surveys Plant Ideas, Document Decisions

Research shows that once people include a charity in their will, they rarely take it out, especially if their gift is properly stewarded, says Frank Robertson, director of planned giving at the University of Minnesota Foundation (Minneapolis, MN).

To reach potential donors and foster a culture of planned estate giving, staff use a version of the generic will survey pictured below.

Sent to prospects identified by the foundation's estate gift predictive model, the survey documents gift commitments already made, which allows new donors to be incorporated into the stewardship process. It also provides a natural way to introduce potential donors to the idea of establishing an estate gift of their own.

[Insert Collegiate Unit Name] WILL SURVEY

To help the [Insert Collegiate Unit Name] better plan for its future, please take a moment to complete this brief survey. Please be assured we will treat this information with the utmost confidentiality and respect.

1. Have you included the University of Minnesota in your will or estate plans?
   ☐ Yes (please proceed to question 3)
   ☐ No
2. If you have not yet made a provision for the University in your will or estate plans, would you consider doing so in the future? ☐ Yes ☐ No (If no, please comment) _____
3. Thank you for including the University of Minnesota in your will or estate plan! If you haven't already informed us, or if your plans have changed, please describe your gift with as much detail as you are comfortable sharing. We recognize that any estate gift is revocable, is subject to unknown future

personal and financial considerations, and can be modified at any time.
College(s) or program(s) you wish to support:
_____
_____

Purpose of gift or area of support (such as scholarships, fellowships, research, etc.):
_____
_____

*Description of your gift (percentage, residuary or fixed amount). For long-term planning purposes it would also be helpful to the University if you could state an estimate of the present value of your gift._____
_____
_____

All donors of future gifts to the University of Minnesota are recognized as members of the Heritage Society of the University of Minnesota Presidents Club, regardless of the amount (or if no amount is stated). We hope you will allow us to recognize your generosity in this way and to list your name(s) as an

inspiration to others. Please indicate how your name(s) should appear on any recognition material and on our annual donor roster:
_____
_____

☐ Please do not list my/our name(s) in any donor rosters or publications.
4. Would you like more information about any of the following? (Check all that interest you):
☐ Testamentary Bequests
☐ Charitable Gift annuities
☐ Gifts of Real Estate
☐ Charitable remainder trusts
☐ Gifts from Retirement plans
☐ Estate Planning Seminars

THANK YOU for taking time to complete this survey! For more information, please contact:
Name
Planned Giving Officer, U of M Foundation
Phone
e-mail

70. Invite Planned Gift Donors to Consider Current Gifts

How many planned gift expectancies — planned gifts you are aware of that will be realized after the donor's lifetime — do you currently have? How many of the persons who have made planned gift provisions are already generously donating to your cause?

If you have confirmed planned gift donors who have given little in the way of outright gifts, explore with them the possibility of establishing a fund now, while they are still living, then adding to it after their lifetimes.

The advantage to them? They can experience the joy of seeing what their gift is accomplishing while they are still alive and be comforted in knowing even more can be done after their lifetime. In addition, they can witness the appropriateness of any restrictions that have been placed on the fund to know whether changes might be in order. An example would be a donor who has established a college scholarship fund for single mothers majoring in education. Upon seeing the scholarship in action, the donor may choose to expand it to other majors as well, an option that wouldn't have existed if the scholarship hadn't become active until after the donor's death.

Although you should approach this topic gently so as not to jeopardize any future planned gift provisions, there is certainly justification for at least exploring the notion of establishing a fund prior to a donor's death.

71. Tool Helps Start, Strengthen a Planned Giving Program

Jerold Panas, of Jerold Panas, Linzy & Partners (Chicago, IL), developed a tool specifically to help organizations start a planned giving program or strengthen an existing one.

Shown at right, the tool, Coming of Age —The Twenty-One Factors in Designing a Successful Planned Giving Program, is divided into two sections, activity and action.

Even if you have a planned giving program in place, Panas recommends reviewing the steps listed in the tool to make sure your program incorporates all of them. "It is most helpful if you have a consultant who can go through all the steps and develop ways to put them into practice," he says.

The action section is used to record when activities are completed. "For example, for the first activity, board approval of a planned giving program, you would put the date the board will be meeting to give approval. Each activity has to be time bonded in order to be effective. If you don't know you have deadlines to meet or hurdles to jump over, there will be no urgency to getting things done."

Source: Jerold Panas, Jerold Panas, Linzy & Partners, Chicago, IL. E-mail: ideas@panaslinzy.com

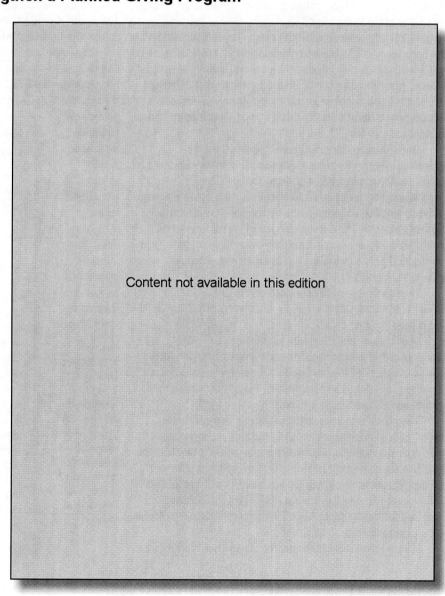

Content not available in this edition

72. Set Confidentiality Parameters

When a donor emphasizes the confidentiality of shared information, clarify the degree to which you are able to discuss matters with other key staff in your organization — just so you're both on the same page.

73. Planned Gifts Triggers

■ Key life events can cause donors to think about planned giving. Events that can trigger the desire for estate planning include the birth of a child or grandchild, the death of a friend or relative or the retirement of the donor.

74. Empower Potential Donors With Estate Planning Seminar

Planned giving is an indispensable part of many nonprofit's fundraising efforts. For prospects and donors, though, estate planning can be a complex and confusing affair. To increase your stakeholders' confidence in arranging their financial affairs — including making provisions for your organization, if they wish — consider offering an estate planning seminar.

Officials at Long Island University (New York, NY) have been reaching out to donors with estate planning seminars for over ten years. "The seminars' primary purpose is to identify qualified leads and to educate the general public," says Cindy March, associate director of planned giving, in explaining why such free-of-charge events make strategic sense. "It's a lot of work, but it's worth it. It's a great stewardship and cultivation exercise."

The two-hour planning events presented by the university's planned giving society are held in the campus's center for the performing arts. Attended by 50 to 75 participants, the program features not only the estate planning presentation, but also an address by the university president. Refreshments and time for socialization are included, and participants receive an information packet that includes flyers on planned giving vehicles such as charitable gift annuities and gifts of real estate.

Though the event is promoted on the university's website, most attendees come from demographics targeted by the planned giving office.

March says invitations are sent to anyone in the development database who is over the age of 50 and lives within 25 miles of the university, all planned giving society members, anyone who has made an inquiry about planned giving and all university retirees.

March says personal touches are key to a successful event, both in boosting attendance and aiding subsequent cultivation efforts. She personally invites close contacts to the seminar, for example. She also greets attendees as they arrive, invites prospects to join her for lunch afterwards and makes follow-up calls after the seminar. This is all in addition to standard follow-up procedures like the comprehensive planned giving brochure sent to all attendees.

How aggressively is the university promoted during the event? "We have a mild emphasis on charitable giving, but we don't hit them over the head with it," March says. "The presenter will use the university in hypothetical examples, and we distribute a survey that, among other things, asks participants if they have included us in their estate plans. But we don't solicit on the spot. Our goal is for participants to learn something, to become motivated and to have the tools to meet with their attorney," she says.

The approach has shown results. One man March took out to lunch — a man who had no history of major giving — established a $25,000 anonymous scholarship and set up two charitable gift annuities. Another woman who had come to multiple planning seminars finally decided to give a gift annuity.

"And for some of these people, this is just the beginning," says March.

Source: Cindy March, Associate Director of Planned Giving, C.W. Post Campus, Long Island University, Brookville, NY. E-mail: cindy.march@liu.edu

How to Find an Estate Planning Seminar Presenter

Long Island University (New York, NY) was lucky, says Cindy March, associate director of planned giving — the lawyer who gives their estate planning seminar was recommended by another organization and is happy to work on a pro-bono basis.

But not every organization will be so lucky, and March recommends getting to know a potential speaker — and going to a presentation to see them in action — before extending a speaking invitation. "Your guests are trusting you, and you don't want to expose some of your most important prospects to an inappropriate experience."

In general, March says presenters should have a solid résumé of estate planning practice and should be able to explain concepts in simple terms without talking down to people. She says it's also important to avoid presenters who treat the seminar as an opportunity to promote their own practice or business.

75. Keep Retiring Board Members In the Fold

Here's the usual pattern: You discover someone with financial capability, take steps to involve him/her in the life of your organization — quite often serving on a committee or advisory council — and then eventually move the individual to your board of directors (or trustees) to serve out as many terms as is possible before the person is retired.

But then what? Is that it?

It doesn't have to be. Rather than putting board members out to pasture, consider reversing the process. Once a

board member retires, offer him/her the opportunity to stay connected with your organization by rejoining one of your committees or advisory groups again. The board member will be much more in tune with what he/she finds most fulfilling about your organization and can select a new point of involvement that will be mutually rewarding.

Besides providing valuable help, former board members will be much more likely to make a major gift, if they're actively engaged in advancement activities.

76. Be Prepared Before Starting a Charitable Gift Annuity Program

With the average charitable gift annuity bringing in over $43,000, annuity programs can be a valuable source of revenue. Administering them, though, is no small task, and Kathryn Miree, president of Kathryn W. Miree & Associates (Birmingham, AL) recommends gathering all the facts before starting one.

"Nonprofits need to know the infrastructure and costs it takes to do a program right, and have realistic expectations about the returns they will see," she says.

Miree shares some advice and insight for organizations looking to establish or improve a charitable gift annuity program.

What kinds of assets should be accepted toward a gift annuity?

"I'm pretty conservative on that — I recommend only cash or marketable securities. This allows you to start investing the funds immediately. If you accept something like real estate or a closely held business, you're liable not only to have a long delay in the sale of the asset, you're subject to market fluctuations. Reducing the assets to cash almost always involves additional expenses as well."

What minimum age do you advise for annuity donors?

"Organizations have become more conservative on this. The minimum for a current annuity might be 60 to 65, while a deferred annuity might be 55 to 60. It also depends on the maturity of the nonprofit. The younger its program and the smaller its annuity pool, the more conservative it should be."

What about minimum donations?

"There is no industry standard, but $10,000 is the minimum I see most often. With all American Council on Gift Annuities (ACGA) assuming a 50 percent residuum on the initial gift, that minimum provides $5,000 to the annuitant and leaves $5,000 for the charity."

How is marketing charitable gift annuities the same as or different from other planned giving vehicles?

"Gift annuities are perfect for donors who want to make a significant donation but are nervous about the economy. But I wouldn't recommend them to anyone who doesn't need an

ongoing revenue stream. Annuities are not a financial product and should not be marketed like one."

What regulatory/legal requirements should an organization be aware of?

"Every state has its own requirements. Some states require you to file with or notify them in addition to sending a 1099R. Some require you to maintain a reserve fund. Some require that reserve to be invested in specific assets or a segregated trust. Almost all states also stipulate specific language that must be included in the gift annuity document. Annuities can be a lot of work, and for that reason I don't advise charities to offer them unless they are willing to commit the resources to do it right."

How do you know if you are ready to offer gift annuities?

"Large organizations that want to be competitive need to offer them, but annuities are not something that every nonprofit needs to be doing. If your charity is so small that you don't have full time development staff and formal gift acceptance policies, there's really no way you can manage a charitable gift annuity program."

Source: Kathryn Miree, President, Kathryn W. Miree & Associates, Birmingham, AL. E-mail: kwmiree@ kathrynmiree andassociates. com

Annuity Mistakes to Avoid

Q. *What mistakes do you see organizations making in setting up or running an annuity program?*

1. "Not being respectful of state regulations. Many think they simply don't need to worry about following the rules."
2. "Accepting things other than cash and marketable securities in order to secure more annuities."
3. "Not marketing their program consistently enough. If you're going to offer an annuity program, my one rule is to make it visible. If you have a program, you don't want to be doing one annuity a year. The more annuities you have, the more the risk is spread around, so you want to build the biggest pool you can."

— *Kathryn Miree, President, Kathryn W. Miree & Associates (Birmingham, AL)*

77. Engage Volunteers in Planned Gift Development

Whether your planned gifts program is simple or sophisticated, engaging volunteers makes good sense. Anything others can do will multiply your planned gift efforts and increase the probability of receiving more planned gifts. Plus, the very act of involving those individuals will increase the likelihood that they will consider planned gifts as well.

Here are some examples of how to involve volunteers in your planned gifts effort:

❑ **Assemble a planned gifts advisory committee** to review (or create) your planned gifts policies and oversee your program. Include agents of wealth (attorneys, trust officers, accountants, insurance agents), planned gift donors and prospects.

❑ **Enlist small committees in key communities/regions.**

Ask participants to serve as ambassadors on your behalf, identifying and cultivating friendships with prospects.

❑ Enlist professionals and friends of your nonprofit to help **conduct an estate planning seminar.**

❑ Ask existing planned gift donors to **write brief articles or offer testimonials** as to why they made the gift. Use in brochures, planned gifts newsletters and at events.

❑ Ask appropriate volunteers or board members to **sign a letter directed to planned gift prospects.**

❑ **Establish a heritage society** coordinated by volunteers to recognize those individuals who have established planned gifts.

78. Work to Identify and Cultivate Children of Wealth

It's common for most nonprofits to focus on those with existing wealth. To lay the groundwork for major gifts that may not materialize for 10 or 20 years, develop a plan aimed at cultivating children of wealth.

Your community is full of individuals in their 30s, 40s and even 50s who are not yet in positions that enable them to make five- or six-figure gifts but will be in 10 or 20 years by virtue of their positions or inherited wealth.

Begin to cultivate those up-and-comers now with a plan that's unique to your organization. Here's one generic scenario that helps illustrate how to do it:

1. Launch some sort of young leaders society that is exclusive to 30- to 50-year-olds who contribute $1,000 or more annually to your organization.

2. Create a steering committee made of those donors who can take ownership in the effort and design a plan catering to the interests of this age group. The steering committee can come up with social activities, member perks, donor recognition ideas, etc.

3. Encourage the committee to establish an annual awards program that recognizes its members in various categories (e.g., professional achievement, philanthropic efforts, volunteer contributions, etc.).

When members turn 51, induct them into a more traditional, inclusive $1,000-and-above gift club. Hold an annual graduation ceremony that welcomes them into the older crowd.

79. Approach Annual $1,000-plus Donors for Planned Gifts

How many annual contributors do you have at the $1,000-and-above level? What percentage of that group has made planned gift provisions for your organization?

Take steps to encourage and reassure those faithful and generous donors that their annual support will continue long after their lifetimes. Approach donors individually with invitations to make a planned gift that — after their lifetimes — will go to establish named endowment funds. Yearly interest from each fund will provide needed annual

operations support (just as their annual contributions had done during their lifetimes).

Example: Assuming a donor had contributed $1,500 each year to your annual fund, it would take an endowment gift of $30,000 or more — based on an estimated 5 percent return — to yield what had been given yearly. In this instance, encourage the donor to consider a planned gift of not less than $30,000 to make certain his/her level of past support continues well into the future.

80. Retained Life Estate Agreements Offer Many Advantages

Gifts of retained life estate — where a donor deeds property to a charity while retaining the right to use it during his/her lifetime — offer many advantages, particularly if a donor has no natural heirs or has numerous heirs scattered across the country, says Donna Roseman David, senior gift planning officer, Hartford Foundation for Public Giving (Hartford, CT).

Roseman David discusses elements that should be part of retained life estate agreements, based on the sample offered by the Hartford Foundation (shown below right):

1. **Donor's right of usage.** Use of the property through the end of one's life is one primary benefit to the donor, says Roseman David. The right also allows charities to receive larger gifts than the donor might otherwise be able to make.

2. **Donor responsibilities.** Properly structured agreements protect the charity from ongoing and upkeep expenses.

3. **Property damage.** This clause obliges the donor to assume repair costs or split insurance payments with the charity. Roseman David says donors usually provide certification of insurance and premium payment by adding the charity as an additional insured party on the policy, ensuring the organization receives copies of all relevant paperwork.

4. **Indemnity.** This clause provides further protection against cost and damages.

5. **Property inspection.** A gift of retained life estate is an asset, and organizations have a responsibility to protect their assets. Because every property and donor is different, she suggests using a professional inspection service prior to accepting the gift to determine the most appropriate type and frequency of inspection.

6. **Property modification.** This clause protects both the donor's right to improve the property and the charity's right to maintain the value of its asset.

7. **Amendment.** While a gift of remainder interest must be made irrevocably to provide the donor with tax advantages, an amendment clause offers both parties a way to refine arrangements regarding inspection, maintenance and such.

Source: Donna Roseman David, Senior Gift Planning Officer, Hartford Foundation for Public Giving, Hartford, CT. E-mail: Ddavid@hfpg.org

How to Never Invoke a Retained Life Estate Agreement

Retained life estate agreements offer clear legal recourse, but suing a major supporter could be a donor relations disaster. Mitigate the risk of such an eventuality by communicating clear gift acceptance policies to the donor and maintaining rigorous due diligence practices, says Donna Roseman David, senior gift planning officer, Hartford Foundation for Public Giving (Hartford, CT):

"Make sure donors are very clear on what they can and can't do with retained life estate gifts. Writing the contract should be nothing more than formalizing conversations you've already had. You also need to have a comprehensive understanding of the donors' financial health. They might be willing to give the gift, but if you feel their financial position would be too precarious as a result, you might not want to accept it."

Content not available in this edition

81. Encourage Donors to Discuss Giving With Their Children

What parents say and do when it comes to charitable giving and volunteering makes a big difference in the charitable activities of their children once those kids grow up, according to research findings being released in detail today. Parental behavior has tremendous influence — more than religion, politics, race, household income, or any other measured factors on the generosity of today's Americans.

These findings are from Heart of the Donor, an in-depth study commissioned by Russ Reid Company of Pasadena, CA, and conducted by Grey Matter Research & Consulting of Phoenix, AZ.

"The data clearly shows that parental behavior has a very substantial correlation with the eventual behavior of children once they are grown," says Ron Sellers, president of Grey Matter Research. "While the research doesn't show an absolute one-to-one correlation, in real terms today's volunteers are 125 percent more likely to have come from parents who encouraged their children to volunteer, and 145 percent more likely to have come from parents who frequently volunteered, than they are to have come from parents who really never did those things."

"Nonprofits can encourage today's donors to talk to their children about giving and volunteering, model the behavior, and share the experience with them," says Lisa McIntyre, senior vice president of Russ Reid Company and an integral part of the study. "The data clearly shows that when these things are done, it has a long-lasting effect on kids."

Parental involvement is stronger than other predictive factors: ethnicity, education, household income, age, and even whether respondents are currently volunteers.

For more info: Heart of the Donor, Ron Sellers, Grey Matter Research (ron@greymatterresearch.com), ((602) 684-6294 cell), or Lisa McIntyre, Russ Reid Company (lmcintyre@russreid.com), ((800) 275-0430 ext. 205).
Add'l findings: http://www.greymatterresearch.com/index_files/ Parental_Influence.htm.

82. Sometimes a Letter of Introduction Is the Best Approach

When making an initial contact with a new major gift prospect, involving someone familiar with both your organization and the prospect is helpful, but not always possible.

In situations where you're the only individual capable of making an introduction, begin with a sincere letter that sets the stage for an appointment. If appropriate, mention that a mutual friend suggested you contact the prospect.

Remember these four additional points as you produce a letter of introduction:

1. To the highest degree possible, tailor your letter to the prospect's interests and personality. This is where having background information is helpful.
2. Remember your primary objective: to have the opportunity to meet face-to-face.
3. Promise to limit your time to an hour or less.
4. Thank prospect(s) in advance for agreeing to meet with you.

This sample letter illustrates how to approach a prospect with whom you have no prior connection.

Content not available in this edition

83. Enormous Affection for Symphony Results in Gift

Sometimes planned gifts are really providential. Just ask Kathy Carroll, President and CEO of The Toledo Symphony (Toledo, OH). Her organization shared a donation of $600,000 with two other Toledo-area organizations, gifted by the estate of a local woman. Carroll says the gift couldn't have come at a better time. "The gift came during a rather robust year, though we were just shy of making our budget work. With Barbara Parsons' gift, we came in $14,000 over our goal."

Carroll says the gift came about by building a relationship around her interest in music. The symphony offers many opportunities for the members of their Legacy Society to get up close and personal with the musicians of the symphony, including brunches and receptions where musicians participate, teach a lesson or share a piece of music they have written. "It's a chance for our patrons to see our musicians in another light. A very serious cello player might be very silly and funny offstage. The events are a way of revealing ourselves when we're not in our tuxedos."

Barbara Parsons apparently took notice of these opportunities, and though Carroll says she was not someone you might normally view as a major donor, she is very representative of the kind of people who can help.

"It's the rank and file people, sitting in the seats, who have an enormous affection for what we do and remember us with the excitement of a child when they do their estate planning."

Source: Kathy Carroll, President and CEO, The Toledo Symphony, Toledo, OH. E-mail: kcarroll@toledosymphony.com

84. Ask Donors to Complete an Intention Form

At the Fred Hutchinson Cancer Research Center (Seattle, WA), an intention form allows planned giving donors to clearly communicate various aspects of their plans in writing, says Lynette A. Klein, senior director of planned giving.

The form is used to gather contact information, gift details, recognition options and options for memorial recognition, as well as the specific amount or percentage of the planned gift (and estimated amount, if applicable).

"A lot of donors include a percentage of what they are donating to a charity or charities in their will," Klein says, "and the value of that percentage can change a lot from the time they fill it out until the gift is made, so many do not include the estimated amount."

The form is available online and in print form, Klein says, noting that while few people currently fill it out online, center officials hope to increase that number as online giving of planned gifts increases.

The print form, shown here, is a four-panel document used by the center's frontline fundraisers and given to anyone seeking information about planned gifts.

"The form is useful in a couple of ways," she says. "It tells donors about the type of information that is helpful for us to know even if they don't fill it out. Others fill it out, which provides us with information that allows us to have a written confirmation of how a donor wishes their gift to be recognized during their lifetime."

The form's primary value to the center, says Klein, is that it allows them to talk to the donor about their recognition options and their wishes for how the gift is used: "I like the form because it lists different recognition options that we can look at with the donor and discuss with them."

Source: Lynette A. Klein, Senior Director of Planned Giving, Fred Hutchinson Cancer Research Center, Seattle, WA. E-mail: lklein@fhcrc.org

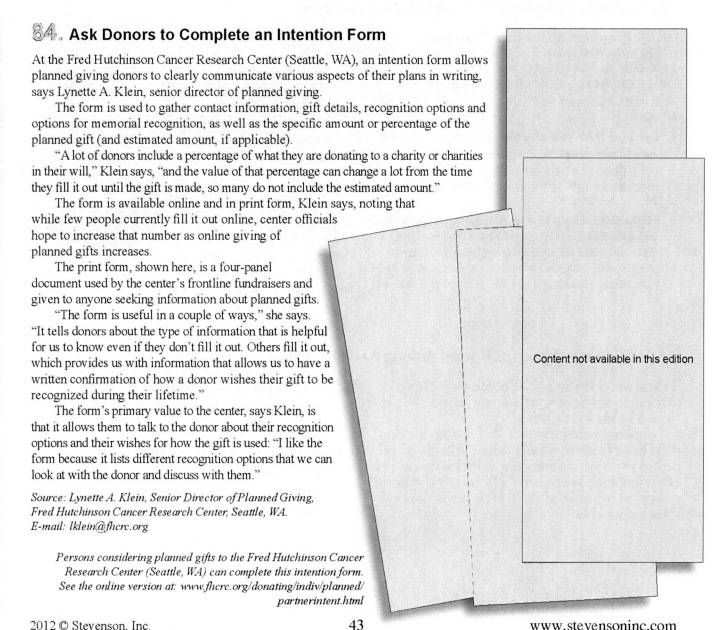

Content not available in this edition

Persons considering planned gifts to the Fred Hutchinson Cancer Research Center (Seattle, WA) can complete this intention form. See the online version at: www.fhcrc.org/donating/indiv/planned/partnerintent.html

85. Five Reasons to Distribute a Planned Gifts Newsletter

Ever wonder if the cost of a planned gifts newsletter is worth it? Here are five reasons it pays to distribute a planned gifts newsletter to select prospects:

1. Those on your mailing list become increasingly knowledgeable about how different types of charitable gifts work and the benefits of each.

2. Regular communication helps position your charity in the minds of those who receive it.

3. Real life examples and illustrations help readers more fully understand the impact of what their own planned gifts might accomplish.

4. The newsletters offer an additional avenue for recognizing those who have made planned gift commitments.

5. By including a return bounce back in every issue of your planned gifts newsletter, you can get answers to important questions such as: Have you included XYZ Charity in your estate plans? Would you like more information about planned gifts to XYZ Charity?

86. Nurture a League of Planned Gift Ambassadors

Although it requires a significant investment of time, building a volunteer group of planned gift ambassadors can significantly increase your ability to identify, cultivate and secure additional planned gifts for your organization.

Here's a framework for building a corps of planned gift ambassadors:

1. **Develop a three-year plan that outlines goals for your ambassador program.** How many volunteers would you like in place at the end of your first year? What communities or geographic locations would be ideal for the presence of these ambassadors?

2. **Methodically begin to recruit, train and support your ambassadors.** Invite those who have already chosen to make a planned gift to serve as ambassadors. Turn to professionals (attorneys, trust officers, insurance agents) in particular communities who have an existing connection to your cause.

3. **Provide your new recruits with a position description that shows what is expected of them** — to regularly identify, research, cultivate and assist in the solicitation of planned gift prospects.

4. **Work with and support each ambassador and ambassador group as circumstances dictate.** Take an ambassador on a call. Accompany an ambassador who is willing to introduce you to a new planned gift prospect. Meet with a community's ambassador group (which may amount to two or three individuals) to review activities and plan strategies.

Even if you have only three ambassador groups with three or four members in each group by the end of year one, you will have launched a volunteer effort that will expand and enhance your efforts to market planned gifts.

87. Make Your Presence Known Among Senior Citizens

If a large part of your responsibility involves marketing planned gift opportunities, then it makes sense to gain greater visibility among senior citizens.

Whether you serve on boards of other organizations or attend public functions, consider those circumstances that position you in senior citizens' circles. For instance, serving as president of a group comprised of many retired individuals places you in a position of respect in the eyes of those with whom you associate.

Here are some additional examples:

❑ Retirement communities and residential settings.

❑ Clubs and civic groups: Kiwanis, Rotary, etc.

❑ Local coffee shops and senior citizen centers.

❑ Churches and synagogues.

❑ Particular social events: travelogue presentations, golfing, bingo gatherings, etc.

88. Planning Ahead Makes for Planned Giving Success

Officials at the American Association of Equine Practitioners (AAEP) Foundation, Lexington, KY, kept planned giving on the back burner for a long time, says Development Coordinator Jodie Bingham. "We had a few gifts come in by luck or circumstance over the past 17 years, but never put a focus on that kind of giving."

That seems ironic, since an estate gift of $225,000 gave the foundation its start. But Bingham says officials wanted to be sure they had laid the internal groundwork needed to ensure there was organizational readiness and commitment to a planned giving program.

So foundation officials spent a year laying that crucial groundwork, says Bingham, along with "making a concentrated effort to let people know we are deserving and ready to accept those kinds of gifts." That effort includes creating the Planned Giving Timeline and Checklist of Essential Actions (below), and Infrastructure Checklist (right).

The timeline/checklist is a one-year plan that led up to the kickoff luncheon of the organization's new Legacy Society that recognizes persons who include the AAEP in estate plans. The checklist details what must be in place to support the society and accept planned gifts.

At the luncheon, foundation officials announced the society's seven charter members, featured the different planned giving options and highlighted the veterinarian who facilitated the original estate gift.

Following this concerted effort, Bingham says foundation officials became prepared to facilitate planned giving by stating key information, highlighting people who are already committed, educating people on how easy planned giving can be and allaying prospects' concerns.

To further educate persons on planned giving, the foundation launched an interactive website (http://www.legacy.vg/aaep/giving/1.html) that allows persons to assess their financial and prospective philanthropic status.

Since the launch of the Legacy Society, Bingham says, they have identified more than $1 million in planned gifts.

Source: Jodie Bingham, Development Coordinator, AAEP Foundation, Lexington, KY. E-mail: jbingham@aaep.org

Content not available in this edition

Content not available in this edition

89. Referral Form Helps Garner Planned Gift Prospects

In what ways do you seek out new planned gift prospects? Do you or have you ever considered using a referral form as one way to identify such individuals?

While it might be inappropriate to utilize a referral form in a mass appeal format, it could certainly prove to be a helpful tool among your centers of influence — planned gift advisory committee, board members, existing planned gift donors and others — as a way to encourage them to assist in your identification effort.

Such referral forms could be distributed on a quarterly or yearly basis to key persons who may be helpful in identifying planned gift prospects.

Use of the referral form stresses the importance of identifying new planned gift prospects and offers a viable way for others to become involved in your planned giving effort.

As you distribute the forms to select individuals, help them understand ideal characteristics of planned gift prospects for your organization. Offer them tips on where to look for such prospects as well. In fact, it may be helpful to give your centers of influence some of the characteristics and circumstances surrounding past planned gift donors to your organization to illustrate the types of individuals who may be prime candidates.

Sample planned gift prospect referral form:

CONFIDENTIAL

WHITLEY
COMMUNITY SCHOOLS
FOUNDATION

Planned Gift Prospect Referral Form

Prospect's Name _____
Address _____
City _____ State _____ ZIP _____
Phone (____) _____ Approximate Age _____
Occupation (or former occupation) _____
Spouse's Name _____
❑ Living ❑ Deceased If living, approximate age _____
Spouse's Occupation _____
Number of Children _____

Children's Names	Location	Occupation

Relationship (if any) to our organization _____

Why do you think this individual might make a good planned gift prospect for our organization?

Why might this individual be inclined to consider a planned gift to our organization?

Would you be willing to assist in introducing a staff person to this individual?

Would you be willing to assist in the cultivation of this individual?

This individual was referred by _____ Date of referral _____

90. All Development Staff Should Help Promote Planned Gifts

The responsibility of planned gifts should not rest with one individual alone.

Each member of the advancement team — in fact, every employee within an organization — can and should assist with this ongoing effort.

Here's a sampling of ways you can encourage persons within your organization to assist with planned giving:

✓ Identify persons within your own circle of friends,

relatives and contacts who may be planned gift prospects, and share their names with your planned gifts officer.

✓ Educate yourself. Meet with the planned gifts officer to learn how you would go about making a personal planned gift to learn more about the process.

✓ Include planned gifts prospects among your calls (after gaining approval from the planned gifts officer).

91. Consider Including a Planned Gift Option in Proposals

When preparing a written proposal for an individual, give thought to including a planned gift provision in addition to the outright gift you are seeking. Why? You have absolutely nothing to lose and much to gain.

Sample language that invites the donor to consider a planned gift in addition to the proposed outright gift:

Including a planned gift component helps the would-be donor consider the long-term affects of the gift he/she is about to make. It lets the donor know that once a pledge is made, that's not necessarily the end. It's a way of showing there's even more the donor could do to have a far greater impact.

> **Suggested Outright Gift: $250,000**
>
> **Planned Gift Consideration**
>
> In addition to your outright gift, we invite you to consider a suitable planned gift as a way to add to this fund after your lifetime (or that of your spouse). There are a variety of planned gift vehicles that could be used to accomplish this goal. We welcome the opportunity to review these options in detail.

92. Make Use of a Charitable Bequest Intent Form

What are you doing to encourage donors to make you aware of their planned gifts? Since it's not uncommon for as few as one-third of a charity's donors to have informed the charitable beneficiary of their bequest, it's important to encourage everyone that it's in their best interest to inform you of their provisions.

To help accomplish that, a charitable bequest intent form is a useful tool. You can share the form with planned gift prospects during one-on-one visits, make the forms available in your planned gifts newsletter, distribute them at key locations and make the form available on your website.

Increase the percentage of planned gift donors who have informed you of their provisions by making use of this form.

Sample bequest intent form:

> **Charitable Bequest Intent**
>
> Please use this form to share the details of your bequest intentions for (Name of Charity). In recognition of your disclosure, we will be honored to invite you to join the (Planned Gifts Recognition Society), a select group of donors who have created a future gift intention for (Name of Charity).
>
> This form is for informational purposes only. Your estate is not legally bound by submitting this statement. It remains revocable and can be modified at any time.
>
> This information will be held in strictest confidence.
>
> Name(s) _____
> Date(s) of Birth _____
> Address_____
> City _____ State _____ ZIP _____
> Phone _____ E-mail _____
>
> **Bequest Specifics**
>
> As evidence of our desire to provide a legacy of support for (Name of Charity), I/we wish to inform (Name of Charity) that you have been named in my/our estate plans.
>
> As of this date, the approximate value of my/our gift is $_____ (If your gift is a percentage of your estate, please indicate the approximate present value of that percentage.) I/we designate this gift to be used for:
>
> ❏ **Unrestricted Support** (where the need is greatest as determined by the (Name of Charity) Board of Trustees)
>
> OR
>
> ❏ **The following department or program:** _____
> _____
>
> **(Name of Planned Gift Society)**
>
> In recognition of your intention, it is our great pleasure to induct you as a member of the (Name of Charity) (Name of Planned Gift Society). This select group comprises those having made a planned gift investment in (Name of Charity).
>
> ❏ **Yes, you may publicize my/our name(s) as members of the** (Name of Planned Gift Society), **which serves as a motivation for others to consider planned gifts in support of** (Name of Charity).
>
> ❏ **I/We prefer my/our intentions to remain anonymous.**
>
> _____ _____ _____
> Donor(s)   Signature(s)   Date
>
> Return completed form to: (Name of Charity, Address)